The Economics of Law

The Economics of Law

Second edition

CENTO VELJANOVSKI

iea

The Institute of Economic Affairs

Second edition published in Great Britain in 2006 by
The Institute of Economic Affairs
2 Lord North Street
Westminster
London SW1P 3LB
in association with Profile Books Ltd

First edition published in 1990 by
The Institute of Economic Affairs

The mission of the Institute of Economic Affairs is to improve public understanding of the fundamental institutions of a free society, by analysing and expounding the role of markets in solving economic and social problems.

A CIP catalogue record for this book is available from the British Library.

ISBN-10: 0 255 36561 6
ISBN-13: 978 0 255 36561 1

Many IEA publications are translated into languages other than English or are reprinted. Permission to translate or to reprint should be sought from the Director General at the address above.

Typeset in Stone by Phoenix Photosetting, Chatham, Kent
www.phoenixphotosetting.co.uk

Printed and bound in Great Britain by Hobbs the Printers

CONTENTS

The author		8
Foreword by Geoffrey E. Wood		10
Summary		14
List of tables, figures and boxes		17

1	**Introduction**	21
	'A harmful disciplinary divide'	22
	The economic approach to law	24
	Outline of the book	25

2	**A short history**	27
	Disciplinary divides	28
	The development of the economic approach	30

3	**Law as an incentive system**	44
	Ex post versus *ex ante*	44
	Rent control and all that	47
	Assumption of economic rationality	49
	Economists do it with models	53
	Positive versus normative economics	56
	Empirical analysis	57
	Law without ethics	58
	Summing up	61

4 The economic approach   62
A biblical parable   62
Economics – choice and scarcity   64
Costs and benefits   64
Coasian economics   72
Implications of opportunity cost analysis   74

5 Some legal applications   78
The roles of the economist   78
Personal injury damages   80
The economics of crime   84
Defining legal terms   93

6 Competition law   106
The rise of the economic approach   107
Why do we need competition law?   113
Defining legal terms   120
Efficiency: goal, defence or offence?   130
Antitrust and the new economy   133
The danger of 'nip and tuck' economics   140
Assessment   141

7 Regulation   143
Models of regulation   145
Regulation as a barrier to competition   151
Adaptive responses to regulation   152
Economics of legal rules   155

Use of cost–benefit analysis   164
Market-based alternatives   169

8 Concluding remarks   173

Questions for discussion   175
Further reading   176

About the IEA   178

THE AUTHOR

Dr Cento Veljanovski is Managing Partner of Case Associates, IEA Fellow in Law & Economics, and an Associate Research Fellow, Institute of Advanced Legal Studies, University of London. He was previously Research and Editorial Director at the Institute of Economic Affairs (1989–91), Lecturer in Law and Economics, University College London (1984–87), Research Fellow, Centre for Socio-Legal Studies, Oxford (1974–84), and has held academic positions at UK, North American and Australian universities. He holds several degrees in law and economics (BEc, MEc, DPhil), and is an Associate Member of the Chartered Institute of Arbitrators (ACIArb). Dr Veljanovski has been in private practice since 1990, providing economic analysis in regulatory and competition investigations, and has appeared as an expert witness is many court cases on competition and damage claims. He was voted one of the most highly regarded competition economists globally in the 2006 Global Competition Review survey.

Dr Veljanovski was the first economist appointed to a lectureship in a law department at a British university. He has written many books and articles on industrial economics, economic reform and law and economics, including *Selling the State: Privatisation in Britain* (1988), *The Economic Approach to Law* (1982) and *Economic Principles of Law* (2007). He is a member of the editorial boards of *United Kingdom Competition Law Reports*,

Journal of Network Industries and *Journal des Economistes et des Etudes Humaines*, and the advisory committees of the Erasmus Programme in Law and Economics, Centre for the Study of the New Institutional Economics (University of Saarland), and the Centre for Law and Economics (Australian National University).

FOREWORD

When the Editorial and Programme Director of the Institute of Economic Affairs asked me to write the foreword to this new edition of Cento Veljanovski's *The Economics of Law*, I accepted his invitation immediately and with great pleasure. A book I had long wanted to see back in print, to benefit both new generations of students and practising lawyers and economists as yet unfamiliar with the area, would soon once again be available.

Dr Veljanovski's book was first published in 1990, and a second impression appeared in 1996. Since then there has been little in the area for the British reader. Introductory texts have been aimed primarily at the US market, a meaningful concept in this context, although not when applied to many other kinds of textbook – while US and English law have common origins there are many differences. Further, these texts have been longer and more detailed than anyone wanting simply a guide to why the subject is so important, and so interesting, would actually need. This substantially revised edition of *The Economics of Law* is therefore greatly welcome.

Why exactly is the subject so important and so interesting? Law and economics are almost inevitably intertwined. In a world with only one person – Robinson Crusoe – economics would still have a role. Crusoe has to decide how much of his time to spend making a better fishing rod, an activity that delays his going to catch fish. Resources, in other words, are always scarce and decisions have to be made about how to allocate them among various activities. In that world there would be no need for law. But give Crusoe a helper – Friday – and immediately law is needed to deal with who can use what. How much is Friday to get for his labours if he is a helper? Or, if he is a neighbour who just happens to find a fish Crusoe has caught, is he entitled to fillet, cook and eat it? The moment there is more than one person in the world, efficient resource allocation requires the definition and enforcement, even if only by custom, of property rights. To see why, consider again Crusoe's fishing rod versus fish decision. If he cannot rely on getting the share he expects of the fish he catches, why should he even consider spending effort to improve his fishing technology?

One role, then, of the discipline of law and economics is to explore whether laws promote economically efficient outcomes and, if they do not, to suggest how they can be changed to do so, always provided the cost of the change falls short of the benefits.

To an extent economists view law as, to quote Dr Veljanovski, 'a giant pricing machine'. This view, he says, 'leads [economists] to a fundamentally different view of law which, while not alien to lawyers, is not central'. In contrast to that, lawyers, he writes, see law as 'a set of rules and procedures'. They take a 'retrospective view', and begin with a dispute that needs to be resolved. It is therefore 'natural that [the lawyer] should focus on the question of how [the dispute] is to be resolved and how the solution affects the welfare of the parties directly involved'.

In Chapter 4, 'The economic approach', it is shown very clearly how this is an apparent rather than a real conflict. Dr Veljanovski's demonstration draws on a famous article by Ronald Coase, which showed that if two parties, each of whom is affected by an action of the other, can negotiate with each other, then however a court decides in a dispute will not matter in terms of what actually happens. Negotiation will lead the parties to the least-cost outcome.

Dr Veljanovski uses this to illustrate some important propositions – economics matters not only when financial costs are involved: mutual incompatibility not 'the physical causation of harm' is the basis of harmful interactions between activities; the law has no allocative effect when transaction costs are trivial; and that when such costs are not trivial the law can have significant effects on 'economic activity and behaviour'.

Economic activity and behaviour, it must be emphasised, includes what we would call crime.[1] Economics can guide us on the combination of penalties and risk of enforcement that brings the least-cost result. How severe, for example, should fines or other sentences be? There is a right answer to that question. It still awaits discovery but, as Dr Veljanovski shows, we can get nearer it with the use of economic analysis than we can without such help.

Economics also extends into the analysis of regulation – very important now as regulation has increased so greatly in Britain in recent years. It can help us analyse and often improve competition law. In these areas we can use economics to appraise and refine parliamentary and regulatory decisions. Further, we can look not only at decisions but also at processes and rules, asking whether these will tend to produce efficient outcomes even in situations

---

1   I do not venture here into discussion of whether crime is a construct of law; but I would maintain that while it is defined by law the definitions have economic foundations. If something is deemed a crime it must be thought to cause harm, and that is a cost. Different societies may, of course, differ over what is harm, and others may think the views of some other societies bizarre. Saying that is not the end of the matter – but going farther would be too substantial a digression.

unknown when the rule or regulation was framed. Economics also has a role in comparatively simple matters, showing how, for example, to calculate appropriate compensation resulting from a decision over liability for harm.

Strikingly, economically efficient outcomes come not only from the conscious application of economic analysis to the framing of laws; law has in many areas evolved towards producing efficient outcomes. This conclusion, startling to some, was argued by Guido Calabrisi in 1967, and then by Richard Posner in a series of papers and books. More details of these, and of the work of the economists who also helped open up the joint study of law and economics, can be found in Chapter 2 of Dr Veljanovski's book.

As I hope I have made clear, this is an important book. It is to be recommended without hesitation to any economist or lawyer who wants to find out about the discipline that combines these two fields of study. I would expect that any such reader would soon be engrossed in a book that is at once enjoyable, well written, informative and useful. And I would predict that any reader who opened it not expecting to be persuaded of the virtues of the approach described and advocated by Dr Veljanovski would soon be reading avidly, and would end the book a convert.

GEOFFREY E. WOOD
Professor of Economics,
Sir John Cass Business School, City University,
Professor of Monetary Economics,
University of Buckingham
August 2006

SUMMARY

- Economic analysis is increasingly applied beyond its traditional precincts of the marketplace and the economy. One area where this has happened is the economic approach to law. This is the application of economic theory, mostly price theory, and statistical methods to examine the formation, structure, processes and impact of the law and legal institutions.
- Economics and the law were connected in the work of many classical economists, but the disciplines became separated until the work of a number of Chicago School economists and public choice theorists in the second half of the twentieth century applied economic analysis to areas that had come to be deemed beyond the realm of economics.
- The economics of law is concerned with laws that regulate economic activity – those laws which affect markets, industries and firms, and economic variables such as prices, investment, profits, income distribution and resource allocation generally – but it also goes well beyond these areas to examine fundamental legal institutions.
- The economics of law stresses that the value of goods and services depends crucially on the 'bundle of legal rights' that

is transferred with them, and that markets trade in these legal rights.

- The law prices and taxes individual human behaviour and therefore influences that behaviour. The economic approach to the law is more concerned with the way the law affects the choices and actions of all potential litigants and individuals likely to find themselves in similar circumstances, rather than the effect of particular legal decisions on the welfare of the parties to a dispute.
- Economics places at the forefront of discussion the costs and benefits of the law, considerations that will always be relevant when resources are finite. All too often, lawyers (as well as politicians, pressure groups and civil servants) discuss the law as if it were costless. Economics informs us that nothing is free from the viewpoint of society as a whole.
- Economics offers a means of evaluating the costs and benefits of different laws by attributing monetary values to different harms, outcomes and consequences. The economist uses the word 'costs' where the lawyer would use 'interests', but the economist's balancing of costs and benefits is no different from the judgmental process engaged in by the courts in resolving most legal disputes.
- Application of the economic approach to competition and antitrust law shows that such law is often founded upon a misunderstanding of the nature of markets, economic efficiency and competition. For example, the EU Commission has often treated innovation as a competition problem and first mover advantage as dominance, yet economic analysis shows that these are natural phenomena that are intrinsic to healthy market competition.

- Economic analysis has also shown that much regulation does not occur simply as a response to market failure, but can often be explained as a result of rent-seeking by already powerful special interests. Moreover, economics can show that regulation is often a barrier to competition and may impose greater costs than the harm it was intended to ameliorate.
- Laws exist for a purpose; they are not ends in themselves. They seek to guide, control, deter and punish. It follows that the study of law must, almost by definition, be broadened to include an understanding of its justification and effects. Economics provides an established approach to examine the justification and effects of the law beyond what may be possible by a conventional legal approach.

TABLES, FIGURES AND BOXES

Table 1   Estimated costs of reducing property crimes
           by 1 per cent   89
Table 2   Average value of prevention per casualty by
           severity and element of cost   166
Table 3   Estimated annual cost savings from mobile
           phone ban   168

Figure 1   The effect on the rate of property crimes of a
           10 per cent increase in five variables   87
Figure 2   The way an economist sees negligence   104
Figure 3   The costs of monopoly   117

Box 1   Law without economics – 'a deadly combination'   23
Box 2   Did economics create humans?   51
Box 3   Economic application of the Hand Test   98
Box 4   Adam Smith in court   109
Box 5   The economic costs of monopoly and rent-seeking   116
Box 6   Pizza – a ssnip at the price?   125

The Economics of Law

1   INTRODUCTION

Increasingly, economics is being extended beyond its traditional precincts of the marketplace and the economy. One endeavour that has gained respectability is the economic approach to law. This is the application of modern price theory and empirical techniques to the analysis, interpretation, assessment and design of laws, legal procedures and institutions.

When the first edition of this Hobart Paper was written in 1990 the economics of law was struggling in Europe, both as an intellectual discipline and as a basis for public policy and legal reform. Today there is a greater awareness of the benefits of private property rights and markets, and the disadvantages and inefficiency of bureaucracy and regulation as means of coordinating the economy. Mainstream economics and legal texts now include economic analyses of the laws and institutions, and there is a greater acknowledgement of the need for and benefits of 'efficient' laws and markets. In some areas, such as utility regulation and competition and merger laws, economics has had a profound effect. The economic approach is not simply seen as just another interesting perspective in these areas of law, but as an essential part of the law itself! This has given a practical impetus for the wider acceptance of the economic approach to areas where the economic content and relevance of economics are not as obvious.

'A harmful disciplinary divide'

It is important not to exaggerate the influence that economics has had on law and lawyers. For far too long an unnecessary and positively harmful disciplinary divide between law and economics has existed and still persists today. Both disciplines suffer from what Veblen called 'trained incapacity'.

Lawyers and policy-makers have generally been economically illiterate and frequently innumerate. The English legal fraternity is wary of theory, contemptuous of experts and academics, and reluctant to accept the idea that other disciplines have something valuable to say about 'law'. To the economist, the approach of lawyers is viewed as excessively descriptive and formalistic. On the occasions when they do venture to comment on legal reform or even the goals and effects of existing laws, their conclusions appear ad hoc rationalisations, ethical and moralistic value judgements or simply assertions based on dubious casual empiricism. The economics editor of the Australian *Sydney Morning Herald* captured the lawyers' approach in the characteristic bluntness of his countrymen when he attacked an Australian Law Reform Commission proposal as:

> ... a highly interventionist remedy, typical of the legal
> mind. It ignores many of the economic issues involved and
> falls back on the lawyer's conviction that all of the world's
> problems can be solved if only we had the right laws. Finding
> a lawyer who understands and respects market forces is as
> hard as finding a baby-wear manufacturer who understands
> and respects celibacy. The legally trained mind cannot grasp
> that it is never possible to defeat market forces, only to
> distort them so they pop up in unexpected ways.[1]

---

1   *Sydney Morning Herald*, 25 May 1981.

Box 1 **Law without economics – 'a deadly combination'**

'Judges move slower than markets but faster than the economics profession, a deadly combination.'

Judge F. Easterbrook (1987)

'A lawyer who has not studied economics ... is very apt to become a public enemy.'

Justice Brandeis (1916)

'... every lawyer ought to seek an understanding of economics. There we are called on to consider and weigh the ends of legislation, the means of attaining them, and the cost. We learn that for everything we have to give up something else, and we are taught to set the advantage we gain against the other advantage we lose and to know what we are doing when we elect.'

Justice O. W. Holmes (1897)

'[Economics] is a powerful, and quite general tool of analysis that everybody who thinks and writes about law uses, consciously or not ... it provides a convenient starting point for a general theory of law in society. It also – and this point must be stressed – has a strong empirical basis, and a basis in common sense. All about us is ample evidence that the system does use its pricing mechanism (in the broadest sense) to manipulate behaviour, and pervasively.'

Professor L. Friedman (1984)

'For the rational study of the law, the black letterman may be the man of the present, but the man of the future is the man of statistics and the master of economics.'

Justice O. W. Holmes (1897)

'Just as other law makers would not dream of now performing their functions in disregard of the economic factor, so courts in their function of declaring, clarifying and extending legal principle must take seriously the economic consequences of what they are doing.'

Justice M. Kirby (2005)

Economists, too, must shoulder considerable criticism. The general inclination was and still is to treat the law as datum. Karl Llewellyn, a noted legal scholar, touched on this many years ago: '… the economist takes … [the law] for granted. Law exists. If it serves economic life well, he has ignored it; if ill, he has pithily cursed it and its devotees, without too great an effort to understand the reason of disservice'.[2]

The economic approach to law

The economics of law can be defined rather crudely as the application of economic theory, mostly price theory, and statistical methods to examine the formation, structure, processes and impact of the law and legal institutions. No consensus has yet emerged, nor do economists possess a unified theory of law. Nevertheless, in the last several decades it has developed into a distinct field of study with its own specialist scholars, journals[3] and texts, with every indication that interest in the field is growing.

---

2   K. N. Llewellyn, 'The effect of legal institutions upon economics', *American Economic Review*, 1925, 13: 665–83.

3   Most notably *Journal of Law and Economics, Journal of Legal Studies, International Review of Law and Economics* and *Journal of Law, Economics and Organization*.

One branch of the economics of law is concerned with laws that regulate economic activity. It examines laws that affect markets, industries and firms, and economic variables such as prices, investment, profits, income distribution and resource allocation generally. It includes competition law (antitrust), industry or utility regulation (the regulation of the privatised utilities and state-owned industries), company, securities, tax, trade, investor and consumer protection laws. This application has grown over the last decade as supply-side reforms have led to the privatisation and liberalisation of industries.

The application of economics to the law is not confined to those areas of law that directly affect markets or economic activity. It goes well beyond these to examine fundamental legal institutions. The more innovative extension of economics is the so-called economics of law or law-and-economics, which takes as its subject matter the entire legal and regulatory systems irrespective of whether or not the law controls economic relationships. It looks in detail at the effects and the structure of the legal doctrines and remedies that make up existing laws. This branch of the economic approach to the law is often seen as synonymous with the analysis of the common law – judge-made law on contract, property and tort (the area of the common law that deals with unintentional harms such as accidents and nuisance) – and family and criminal laws, and many other areas such as legal procedure.

Outline of the book

This Hobart Paper provides an overview of the essential ingredients of the economic approach to law and examples of its applications. The discussion begins in Chapter 2 by briefly outlining the development of the economic approach to law. In Chapter 3 the differences between economic and legal reasoning are discussed. It shows that the economist sees law as a 'giant pricing machine' – laws act as prices or taxes – which provides incentives that affect behaviour and actions – rather than sharing the lawyers' perspective of law as a set of rules and remedies. It is this perspective which marks out the economists' contribution to legal analysis. Chapter 4 sets out the basic 'tools' of the economic approach, most notably the theory of rational choice that underpins the economists' incentive analysis, and the concepts of opportunity costs and economic efficiency, which are central to the economic theory of law and which allow economists to quantify the costs and benefits of laws and legal change. The economic approach is then applied to the calculation of personal injury damages, torts and crime (Chapter 5). This is followed by an overview of the economic approach to competition law (Chapter 6), and regulation, i.e. public and administrative laws (Chapter 7).

2   A SHORT HISTORY

The marrying of economics and law is not new. 'Economic' approaches to law can be found in the utilitarianism of Cesare Bonesara (1764)[1] and Jeremy Bentham (1789);[2] the political economy of Adam Smith (1776)[3] and Karl Marx (1861);[4] and the American Institutionalist school most associated with the work of John R. Commons (1929).[5] Indeed, contemporary economics as a subject grew out of the moral and political philosophy of Adam Smith, the founder of modern economics. Smith's *Wealth of Nations* was only part of a more general theory embracing moral philosophy, economics and the law.[6] Anglo-American common law was also profoundly affected by the political economy of the eighteenth century. Judges, politicians and political economists formed an intellectual circle in which views were openly discussed and shared, and one sees in many legal judgments and judicial writings of the period an appreciation, if not the application, of the economic approach of the time.

1   C. Bonesara, *An Essay in Crime and Punishment*, 1764.
2   J. Bentham, *An Introduction to the Principles of Morals and Legislation*, 1789.
3   A. Smith, *The Wealth of Nations*, 1776.
4   K. Marx, *Das Kapital*, 1861.
5   J. R. Commons, *Legal Foundations of Capitalism*, Macmillan, New York, 1924.
6   His *Lectures on Jurisprudence* were, unfortunately, never completed.

Disciplinary divides

Despite this pedigree, the economic study of law and institutions fell into disrepute among Anglo-American economists and lawyers particularly after World War II. The economists' neglect can be attributed to two principal factors. First, many North American economists associated the study of law and organisations with Institutionalism, which they viewed as overly descriptive, and little more than a school of criticism that lacked a coherent theory. Thus, in 1959, Henry Houthakker, a respected economist, was able to write:

> The economic analysis of institutions is not highly regarded or widely practised among contemporary economists. The very word 'institution' now carries unfavourable associations with the legalistic approach to economic phenomena that were respectable during the first three decades of this century. There is little reason to regret the triumphant reaction that swept institutionalism from its dominant place. Nevertheless, economics can still learn much from the study of institutions. The analytical problems that arise are often both a challenge to conventional theory and a useful reminder of the relativity of accepted doctrine.[7]

The second reason for the economist's neglect lies in the transformation of economics from an a priori to an empirical science. The growing influence of positivism in economics, coupled with the increasing use of mathematics[8] and statistical analysis,

---

7 H. S. Houthakker, 'The scope and limits of futures trading', in M. Abramovitz et al. (eds), *Allocation of Economic Resources*, Stanford University Press, California, 1959, p. 134.

8 Samuelson's classic article on public goods illustrated in three pages the power of mathematics: P. A. Samuelson, 'The pure theory of public expenditure', *Review of Economics & Statistics*, 1954, 36: 387–9.

directed the economist's attention to areas of research where 'hard' data could be found. Institutions and law appeared to defy both mathematical modelling and easy empirical analysis, and were therefore ignored.

Indeed, the mathematical approach progressively took precedence over empirical analysis, as economics become a mathematical fantasia where the honours went to those versed in calculus, topology, set theory, game theory, linear algebra and the like. 'Page after page of the professional economic journals', observed Wassily Leontief, a Nobel Prize-winner in economics, in the early 1980s, 'are filled with mathematical formulae leading to precisely stated but irrelevant conclusions.'[9] The view was shared by one of the founders of modern institutional economics, Ronald Coase, who once quipped: 'In my youth it was said what was too silly to be said may be sung. In modern economics it may be put into mathematics.'[10]

Among lawyers the reluctance to engage in interdisciplinary teaching and research arose from more pragmatic considerations. The first, and perhaps principal, reason is the influence exerted by practitioners on legal education. Law, unlike economics, is a profession. A law degree is a professional qualification primarily designed to equip the student for legal practice, and hence legal education in the UK and most other countries must train the lawyer to ply his or her trade. Indeed, before World War II many English university law courses were taught by part-time practising lawyers. The subservience of the study of law to the demands of the practising profession in the UK placed severe limitations on

9   *The Economist*, 17 July 1982.
10 R. H. Coase, *The Firm, the Market and the Law*, University of Chicago Press, Chicago, 1988.

the ability of legal education to explore the wider context of the law, and bred hostility towards attempts to broaden the base of legal education. Second, legal education, particularly the case method which requires students to study hundreds of cases, is not conducive to the ready acceptance of the social science approach, which seeks to identify generalities rather than the peculiarities of cases that fascinate the legal mind.

The development of the economic approach

The 1960s and 1970s were the formative decades of the law-and-economics movement. During this period a number of separate but related efforts occurred largely within the economics profession which reflected a growing dissatisfaction with the ability of economics to adequately explain basic features of the economy and the way that the economy and industry worked. These centred both on extending economics to explain the nature and effects of regulation, and reformulating the basic conceptual structure of economics itself. It is interesting to note that apart from the work of Guido Calabresi, the building blocks of the economics of law had little to do with explaining and understanding law, and a lot to do with improving the economists' understanding of how the economic system works.

The Chicago School

The growing interest in law-and-economics is intimately associated with, though by no means confined to, the writings of members of the law and economics faculties of the University of Chicago. The 'Chicago School's' approach to economics and law is hard to define in any specific way, although many have cast it in an ideological hue as 'free market economics'. Most would agree, however, that its hallmark is the belief that simple market economics has extraordinary explanatory power in all fields of human and institutional activity. It applies the simple tenets of rational maximising behaviour to all walks of life to elicit testable propositions about the way people and institutions will react to changes in their environment, and to construct proposals for legal reform based on the criterion of economic efficiency.

The work of Gary Becker best epitomises this approach, even though its focus has not been law. Beginning with the economic analysis of labour market discrimination, Becker has applied economics to a wide variety of non-market behaviour such as crime (see Chapter 5), politics, education, the family, health and charity.[11]

The Chicago programme in law-and-economics dates back to the early 1940s when Henry Simons was appointed to the law faculty. After Simons's death in 1947, Aaron Director took over his teaching responsibilities and in 1949 was appointed professor in economics in the Law School. Director exerted a considerable intellectual influence on the economics of antitrust through the work of his students, such as Bowman, Bork and Manne,[12] which was later taken up by Posner, Easterbrook, Landes and others. The Chicago School of antitrust has had a profound effect not only on

---

11 G. S. Becker, *The Economics of Discrimination*, University of Chicago Press, Chicago, 1957; G. S. Becker, *The Economic Approach to Human Behavior*, University of Chicago Press, Chicago, 1976; G. S. Becker, *A Treatise on the Family*, Harvard University Press, Cambridge, MA, 1981.

12 Two important statements of Chicago antitrust economics are R. H. Bork, *The Antitrust Paradox – A Policy at War with Itself*, Basic Books, New York, 1978; R. A. Posner, *Antitrust Law – An Economic Perspective*, University of Chicago Press, Chicago, 1976.

thinking about the purpose of competition law, but also on the law itself (Chapter 6). Its impact was felt elsewhere, particularly in corporate and securities law, such as in Henry Manne's development of the concept of the 'market for corporate control', and more controversially his defence of insider trading.[13] The work on the law and economics of antitrust, coupled with the problem-solving orientation of Chicago economists, provided the impetus for a more general economic study of law. In 1958, the law-and-economics programme at Chicago entered a new phase with the founding of the *Journal of Law and Economics* under the editorship first of Aaron Director and then of Ronald Coase.

Public choice and regulation

In the 1960s a small group of economists studying fiscal policy and taxation began to question the relevance of orthodox economics. The prevailing 'market failure' approach simply did not yield policy proposals that governments followed, nor did it explain the behaviour of bureaucrats and politicians. These economists, drawing on the work of earlier Continental economists such as Wicksell, Lindahl and others, began to incorporate government and bureaucracy into their models.

This led to the development of public choice, or the 'economics of politics' (also known as the 'Virginia School'). Public choice theorists, such as James Buchanan and Gordon Tullock, made government behaviour subject to the same self-regarding forces as those found in markets. Beginning with Downs's *An Economic*

---

13 H. G. Manne, 'Mergers and the market for corporate control', *Journal of Political Economy*, 1965, 73: 110–20; H. G. Manne, *Insider Trading and the Stock Market*, Free Press, New York, 1966.

Theory of Democracy[14] and Buchanan and Tullock's *The Calculus of Consent*,[15] economists began to explain political and bureaucratic behaviour by building on the economic postulate that politicians and civil servants are principally motivated by self-interest. This work had both normative (what should be) and positive (what is) limbs. Normative public choice theory sought to set out legitimate limits to the state in a free society based on individualistic principles and constitutions. Positive public choice sought to develop explanatory theories, most notably the theory of rent-seeking,[16] and to test these against the facts and more rigorous statistical analysis.

The increasing importance of government intervention in the US economy led other economists to model and measure the effects of regulation on industry. The classic articles by Averch and Johnson,[17] Caves,[18] and Stigler and Friedland[19] published in the 1960s mark the beginning of the rigorous and quantitative attempts by economists to model public utility regulation, and more importantly to determine the impact of these laws. Another landmark was Alfred Kahn's *The Economics of Regulation*, published in two volumes in 1970 and 1971.[20]

14　Harper & Row, New York, 1957.

15　University of Michigan Press, Ann Arbor, 1962; G. Tullock, *The Vote Motive*, IEA, London, 1976.

16　G. Tullock, 'The welfare cost of tariffs, monopoly, and theft', *Western Economics Journal*, 1967, 5: 224–32.

17　H. Averch and L. Johnson, 'Behavior of the firm under regulatory constraint', *American Economic Review*, 1962, LII: 1052–69.

18　R. Caves, *Air Transport and Its Regulators: An Industry Study*, Harvard University Press, Cambridge, MA, 1962.

19　G. J. Stigler and C. Friedland, 'What can regulators regulate?: the case of electricity', *Journal of Law and Economics*, 1962, 5: 1–16.

20　A. E. Kahn, *The Economics of Regulation: Principles and Institutions*, vol. I (1970), vol. II (1971); reprinted by MIT Press, Cambridge, MA, 1988.

George Stigler[21] and others went farther to develop a positive theory to explain the nature and growth of regulation. Stigler argued that governments were unlikely to be interested in economic efficiency or some broadly defined concept of the public interest. His central hypothesis was that regulation was secured by politically effective interest groups, invariably producers or sections of the regulated industry, rather than consumers. 'As a rule', argued Stigler, 'regulation is acquired by industry and is designed and operated primarily for its benefit by redistributing income in favour of the regulated industry in return for electoral support for politicians who engineer the redistribution.' Stigler's 'capture theory', together with work in the area of public utilities, stimulated economists in the 1970s to undertake empirical studies of the effects of regulation on industrial performance.

Property rights theory

The early work on property rights by Alchian[22] and Demsetz[23] added an explicit institutional dimension to the extension of economics. Economic theory had hitherto operated in an institutional vacuum, focusing on the production, distribution and consumption of physical goods and services. Property rights theorists stressed that the value of goods and services depends

21 G. J. Stigler, 'The theory of economic regulation', *Bell Journal of Economics and Management Science*, 1971, 2: 3–21.

22 A. A. Alchian, *Some Economics of Property Rights*, Rand Paper no. 2316, Rand Corporation, Santa Monica, CA, 1961; *Pricing and Society*, IEA, London, 1967.

23 H. Demsetz, 'Some aspects of property rights', *Journal of Law and Economics*, 1964, 9: 61–70; 'Toward a theory of property rights', *American Economic Review*, 59: 347–59; 'Toward a theory of property rights II: the competitiveness between private and collective ownership', *Journal of Legal Studies*, 1969, 31: S653–S672. Also Y. Barzel, *Economic Analysis of Property Rights*, 2nd edn, Cambridge University Press, Cambridge, 1997.

crucially on the 'bundle of legal rights' transferred with them, and that markets trade in these legal rights. Clearly, the price of a freehold property differs from that of a leasehold or tenancy, and these different types of ownership arrangements affect the value of land and the efficiency with which it is used. Property rights theorists sought to redefine economics as the study of how variations in 'bundles of property rights' affected prices and the allocation of resources. The approach also identified market failure with the absence of enforceable property rights, and specifically common or open access resources which allowed the overexploitation of the environment, oceans and natural resources. This led to property rights solutions in place of so-called command-and-control intervention to curb overuse and maximise efficiency.

Property rights theorists went farther to posit a dynamic theory of legal evolution and development. Their models 'predicted' that the creation and development of property rights were influenced by economic considerations. In a dynamic economy, new cost-price configurations are generated which provide an opportunity for restructuring, and in particular 'privatising', property. Thus, all other things being equal, the more valuable the prospective property rights, or the lower the costs of defining and enforcing new rights, the more likely it is that new rights will be defined.[24]

Coase and cattle

Perhaps the most important contribution of this period to the conceptual foundations of the economic approach to law and economics itself was Ronald Coase's 'The problem of social costs',[25]

---

24 F. A. Hayek, *Law, Legislation, and Liberty*, 3 vols, University of Chicago Press, Chicago, 1973–9.

25 *Journal of Law and Economics*, 1960, 3: 1–44.

published in 1960. Coase, although not a lawyer, used legal cases to develop several themes that were central to economic theory, and helped bridge the gap between law and economics, although the latter was not his purpose.

The primary purpose of the paper was to correct what Coase saw as a fundamental flaw in the way economists approached questions of public policy.[26] Economists had hitherto given policy advice on the basis of the concept of market failure. Typically, a departure from a model of a perfectly competitive market constituted a prima facie case for government intervention (often referred to as the Pigovian approach after A. C. Pigou, an early-twentieth-century economist). In this analysis government was treated as a costless corrective force, solely concerned with the pursuit of economic efficiency or the public interest. Coase objected to this view, arguing that realistic policy could be devised only if each situation was subjected to detailed investigation based on comparing the total costs and benefits of actual and proposed policy alternatives. In practice both the market and the non-market solutions were imperfect and costly, and these had to be dealt with on an equal footing when deciding which policy to pursue. This is not what economists habitually did, nor do many do so now. As Coase emphasised in 'Social costs', and his earlier equally influential paper on the nature of the firm,[27] the reason why markets appeared to fail was because they were costly to use, i.e. they had high transactions costs. Similarly, government intervention had

26 Coase's paper is the most cited paper in US law journals, outstripping the next most cited article two to one; F. R. Shapiro, 'The most-cited law review articles revisited', *Chicago Kent Law Review*, 1996, 71: 751–79.

27 R. H. Coase, 'The theory of the firm', *Economica*, 1937, 4: 386–405; reprinted in R. H. Coase, *The Firm, the Market and the Law*, University of Chicago Press, Chicago, 1988.

imperfections, costs and created distortions, and was justified only if these were less than the transactions costs of using the market and generated net benefits. The relevant comparison was not between ideals but between feasible, imperfect and costly alternatives. This set the scene for a 'government failures' framework comparable to that of market failure, or what Harold Demsetz was later to call the 'comparative institutions approach'.[28]

Coase's article is famous for another reason. He elaborated a proposition that later became known as the 'Coase Theorem', using trespassing cattle as an example, and further illustrated by English and US nuisance cases. Coase argued that the legal position on whether a rancher or a farmer should be 'liable' for the damages caused by trespassing cattle trampling wheat fields would not affect the efficient outcome provided that transactions costs were zero. The Coase Theorem holds that in a world where bargaining is costless, property rights will be transferred to those who value them the highest. Moreover, Coase claimed that the amount of damaged wheat would be the same whether the law held the rancher liable for the damages or not, provided that the parties could get together to bargain relatively cheaply. The only impact of the law was on the relative wealth of individuals. That is, potential gains-from-trade, and not the law, determined the allocation of resources. This counter-intuitive conclusion and its implication for policy analysis are explained in more detail in Chapter 4.

Coase, like property rights theorists, also stressed that the presence of positive transactions costs could help explain otherwise puzzling economic and institutional features of the

28 H. Demsetz, 'Information and efficiency: another viewpoint', *Journal of Law and Economics*, 1969, 12: 1–22.

economy. The development of contracts, laws and institutions could be seen as attempts to economise on transactions costs where they were a less costly way of organising economic activity.

Calabresi's costs of accidents

An article by Guido Calabresi, then of Yale University, titled 'Some thoughts on risk distribution and the law of torts',[29] was the first systematic attempt by a lawyer to examine the law of torts from an economic perspective. Calabresi argued that the goal of accident law was to 'minimise the sum of the costs of accidents and the costs of preventing accidents'. He later refined this axiom into a theory of liability for accident losses. According to Calabresi, the costs of accidents could be minimised if the party that could avoid the accident at least cost was made liable for the loss. This Calabresi called the 'cheapest-cost-avoider' rule.[30] His idea is simple to illustrate (ignoring for simplicity the random nature of accidents). A careless driver's car collides with a pedestrian, inflicting expected damages totalling £200. It is discovered that the accident resulted from the driver's failure to fit new brakes costing £50. Clearly, road users and society as a whole would benefit if the driver had fitted new brakes, the benefit being £150 (equal to the avoided loss of £200 minus the cost of the new brakes, £50). If the driver is made legally liable for the loss – that is, he is required to pay the victim compensation of £200 should an accident occur – then clearly he

---

29   *Yale Law Journal*, 1967, 70: 499–553.

30   G. Calabresi, *The Costs of Accidents: A Legal and Economic Analysis*, Yale University Press, New Haven, 1970. Calabresi's work was introduced to a British audience in P. S. Atiyah, *Accidents, Compensation and the Law*, Weidenfeld & Nicolson, London, 1970.

would have a strong incentive to fit the new brakes. A liability rule that shifts the loss whenever it would encourage careless drivers to fit new brakes makes the efficient solution the cheapest solution for the driver.

The distinctive quality of Calabresi's work was to show the power of simple economic principles to rationalise a whole body of law, and to develop a coherent normative basis for its reform.

Posner's efficiency analysis

The next two decades were the growth period of the law-and-economics movement, perhaps peaking in the mid-1980s in the USA.[31] Increasingly, North American legal scholars began to use economics to rationalise and appraise the law, and by the end of the 1980s the law-and-economics movement had firmly established itself as a respectable component of legal studies.

If one personality had to be chosen to represent this period, it would be Richard Posner, then of the University of Chicago Law School (now Chief Judge of the US Court of Appeals).[32] Although Posner's work remains controversial, there is no doubt that his contributions are both important and durable.

Posner demonstrated that simple economic concepts could be used to analyse all areas of law – contract, property, criminal, family, commercial, constitutional, administrative and procedural laws. His treatise, *Economic Analysis of Law*, first published in 1973 and now in its sixth edition, is a tour de force of subtle (and sometimes not so subtle) and detailed applications of economics to

---

31 W. M. Landes and R. A. Posner, 'The influence of economics of law: a quantitative study', *Journal of Law and Economics*, 1993, 36: 385–424.

32 R. A. Posner, *Economic Analysis of Law*, Little, Brown, Boston, MA, 1977 (6th edn, 2003).

law. Posner has shown that many legal doctrines and procedural rules could be given economic explanation and rationalisation. This type of economic analysis of law (which is discussed further in Chapter 4) attempts to explain the nature of legal doctrines using the concept of economic efficiency. While this approach is fraught with difficulties, Posner's work, beginning with his paper 'A theory of negligence',[33] and refined in an impressive sequence of articles and books, ushered in a new branch of economic analysis of law, one that the lawyer could use to discover the basis of the hotchpotch of doctrines that make up the common law.

Posner rose to prominence, even notoriety, and captured the imagination of a generation of scholars by going farther to advance the radical thesis that the fundamental logic of the common law was economic. He argued that judges unwittingly decided cases in a way that encouraged a more efficient allocation of resources. To the economist, this claim is remarkable for two reasons – judges typically ignore and occasionally reject economic arguments and, when they do employ economics, it is invariably incorrect. To lawyers the complete absence of any reference to economics in decided cases was enough to reject the claim outright. Yet Posner argued that they used, albeit unwittingly, an 'economic approach', and that economics could 'explain' legal doctrines even though these doctrines purported to have no explicit economic basis.

1980 to date

By the mid-1980s the economics of law was a firmly established feature of legal studies in North America. In the USA many of the

---

33   *Journal of Legal Studies*, 1972, 1: 28–96.

prominent scholars in the field (Posner, Bork, Easterbrook, Scalia and Breyer, and later Calabresi) were all 'elevated' to the bench under President Reagan's administration. In 1985 Professor (now Judge) Frank Easterbrook was able to claim that: 'The justices [of the US Supreme Court] are more sophisticated in economic reasoning, and they apply it in a more thoroughgoing way, than at any time in our history.'[34]

Economists were also becoming prominent in the area. Many, such as William Landes, Mitch Polinsky, Steven Shavell and George Priest, were appointed to law schools; law-and-economics programmes and courses sprang up in the top universities; and there was an active programme organised by Henry Manne teaching US lawyers and judges economics. Today most standard economics textbooks contain considerable analysis of law ranging from property rights and liability rules (Coase Theorem) to detailed analysis of contract and criminal laws.[35] This trend is also evident in legal texts and casebooks, which often integrate the economic perspective in the discussion of cases.[36]

There has also been a broadening out into different 'schools', such as the New Institutionalist Economics (NIE) most

---

34 F. Easterbrook, 'Foreword: The court and the economic system', *Harvard Law Review*, 1984, 98: 45.

35 In March 1993 the *Journal of Economic Literature* of the American Economics Association added 'Law and Economics' as a separate classification, formally recognising it as a distinct field of research.

36 H. G. Beale, W. D. Bishop and M. P. Furmston, *Casebook on Contract*, 4th edn, Butterworths, London, 2001; D. Harris, D. Campbell and R. Halson, *Remedies in Contract and Tort*, 2nd edn, Cambridge University Press, Cambridge, 2002; A. Clarke and P. Kohler, *Property Law – Commentary and Materials*, Cambridge University Press, Cambridge, 2005; B. Cheffins, *Company Law – Theory, Structure and Operation*, Clarendon Press, Oxford, 1997.

associated with the work of Oliver Williamson,[37] behavioural law-and-economics, which applies decision theory to create more descriptive models of individual decision-making, and 'post-Chicago economics', which has had a significant impact on competition law.[38] There has also been a resurgence in comparative economics,[39] the study of different economic systems, as a result of the privatisation of the state sector in Western economies and the fall of communism. These approaches draw on the core principles of economics but emphasise different considerations to generate alternative views of the interplay between law, institutions and economics.

At the same time the economic approach has spread across Europe, as shown by the development of specialist law and economics journals and courses.[40] In the civil law countries of Europe,[41] however, and even in the UK with its common law system, the economics of law has not made the same inroads on

37 O. E. Williamson, *The Economic Institutions of Capitalism*, Free Press, New York, 1985; O. E. Williamson, 'The New Institutional Economics: taking stock, looking forward', *Journal of Economic Literature*, 2000, 38: 595–613; International Society for New Institutional Economics (www.isnie.org).

38 C. R. Sunstein (ed.), *Behavioral Approach to Law and Economics*, Cambridge University Press, Cambridge, 2000; F. Parisi and V. L. Smith (eds), *The Law and Economics of Irrational Behavior*, Stanford University Press, Stanford, CT, 2005.

39 S. Djankov et. al., 'The new comparative economics', *Journal of Comparative Economics*, 2003, 31: 595–619.

40 Such as the Erasmus Programme in Law and Economics involving the universities of Bologna, Hamburg, Rotterdam, Ghent, Hamburg, Aix-en-Provence, Haifa, Linköping/Stockholm, Madrid, Manchester and Vienna. See www.frg.eur.nl/rile/emle/universities/index.html.

41 R. van den Bergh, 'The growth of law and economics in Europe', *European Economic Review*, 1996, 40: 969–77.

legal education and scholarship as in the USA.[42] One reason is that judges in these countries are appointed from practising trial attorneys (principally barristers) and not from university law professors as in the USA. Nonetheless, the last decade has seen significant developments that have placed the economic approach at the forefront of legal reform and enforcement. These include the growing concerns over the growth and costs of regulation and its adverse effect on the competitiveness and productivity of the economy, the modernisation of EC competition and merger laws, which have adopted an 'economic approach', and introducing private enforcement and appeals that have brought the courts into the process and often into conflict with regulators.

42   K. G. Dau-Schmidt and C. L. Brun, 'Lost in translation: the economic analysis of law in the United States and Europe', *Columbia Journal of Transnational Law*, 2006, 44: 602–21.

3 LAW AS AN INCENTIVE SYSTEM

It is apparent to any observer that lawyers and economists think and argue in radically different ways. Legal reasoning proceeds by example, argument and the interpretation and meaning of words. Lawyers are trained to distinguish and interpret legal opinions, identify salient facts and apply the law to those facts. Backed into a corner, the lawyer, the judge and most policy-makers will claim that an understanding of economics is not useful. It is confusing, they argue, because economists disagree with one another (ask two economists and you might get three opinions), reach no clear conclusion (if all the economists were placed end to end, they would not reach a firm conclusion), the economy is in a mess, and, in any case, the law pursues goals that in the main are not economic in character. In this chapter the difference between economic and legal reasoning is identified.

Ex post versus *ex ante*

Economists see law as a system for altering incentives; lawyers see it as a set of rules and procedures. This is a fundamental distinction.

Lawyers typically take a retrospective view. Their factual inquiry begins with a dispute that must be resolved by the application of legal principles as distilled from the decisions in past cases. Since the lawyer comes to a problem after the dispute has arisen, it is natural that he should focus on the question of how it is to be resolved and how the solution affects the welfare of the parties directly involved.

There is an overwhelming tendency for lawyers and laymen to treat law as a set of rules and procedures, which can distort the perception of its impact. The law, for example, bans a certain substance or awards compensation to victims according to stated principles that provide full compensation. Reaching for legal textbooks to learn about how law affects individuals is about as much use as reading *The Communist Manifesto* to gain an understanding of the economics, politics and eventual collapse of communism. Knowledge of the law is only the first incomplete step to understanding its structure and effects.

The economist, on the other hand, is not concerned with the effect of the decision on the welfare of the parties to a dispute, but the way the law affects the choices and actions of all potential litigants and individuals likely to find themselves in similar circumstances. His factual inquiry starts well before the dispute, when both parties had the opportunity to reorganise their activities so as to minimise the possibility of a dispute, and the costs and harm that it would inflict. The law is seen as a method of reallocating losses to provide incentives to people to reduce harm and use resources more efficiently.

Once it is recognised that the judge and the legislator can influence the allocation of resources, legal judgments and regulations can be examined for their incentive effects.

Consider the central matter raised in a negligence case that involves the legal liability for accidentally caused losses. In such a case, the issue confronting the courts usually involves a past loss – for example, a negligent driver fails to stop at a red light and damages another vehicle. This loss cannot, obviously, be avoided. It can only be shifted by the judge. But the judicial shifting of losses has effects on future victims and injurers, either by altering their behaviour or their post-injury decision on whether to litigate or settle the case out of court. Thus, while the lawyer will focus on the actions of the parties to an accident to allocate 'fault', the economist will examine the impact of the way the court's decisions affect the accident rate, accident costs and the court's caseload. Moreover, the way the law alters behaviour is often not directly observed by the lawyer, nor indeed is it part of the lawyer's experience. If the law is successful in deterring wrongdoing, accidents or crime, it means a legal dispute has been avoided. In short, successful laws mean less business for lawyers. It is therefore not surprising that they should give this part of the law less attention.

This simple difference of view explains a large part of the gap between economic and legal reasoning. Lawyers are concerned with the aftermath of the disputes and conflicts that inevitably occur in society. The economist is concerned with the effect that rules have on behaviour *before* the mishap has occurred. The economist normally thinks of altering and tilting the incentives confronting individuals. In short, to quote Lawrence Friedman: 'The basic idea of economic theory is that the legal system is a giant pricing machine ... When laws grant rights, or impose duties, they make behaviour of one sort or another cheaper or more expensive.'[1]

---

1   L. M. Friedman, 'Two Faces of Law', *Wisconsin Law Review*, 1984, 1: 13–33.

Rent control and all that

Perhaps the best-documented example of the incentive effects of law is price controls, and rent control in particular. The belief underlying rent control legislation is that by reducing rents government can assist the poorer members of society to obtain cheaper 'affordable' accommodation. But economics informs us that reducing the price of a good or service below the market price simply creates greater shortages and inefficiencies. This is because at the lower rents imposed by the controls landlords reduce the supply of rented accommodation while at the same time more people want to rent because it is cheaper. Thus rent control temporarily benefits those lucky enough to be tenants but at a 'cost' of increasing the shortages that prompted the controls in the first place.

Rent control also has a series of second-round or ripple effects. If it persists then progressively more and more rentable properties will be withdrawn from the market. Second, because landlords get less rent they will look for other ways of increasing the income from their properties. They will, initially, try to get around controls by requiring 'key' or 'deposit' money from those prepared to pay to 'jump' the long queues for the limited number of flats and houses that are offered to tenants, or impose repair and maintenance obligations on tenants. If these terms are also controlled, landlords will either withdraw their properties or allow them to deteriorate. Landlords will also be much more selective in their choice of tenants in an effort to avoid 'bad' tenants who might damage or not look after the accommodation and/or who pose a high risk of defaulting on paying rent. There will also be a greater likelihood of discrimination as landlords use race, sex, education, marital status and just pure prejudice to select a tenant. The non-rent costs to prospective tenants will also rise. They will have to wait longer to find accommodation, and incur greater search and other costs. The net result of rent control legislation is greater shortages, less affordable decent-quality accommodation, more homeless people and greater social discord and unhappiness. The unintended effects would progressively overwhelm its intended effect. It is therefore not surprising that this type of legislation has largely disappeared.

Take another example – people who get themselves into too much debt. Today the levels of personal and national debt have risen significantly, and many people and countries have found themselves unable to make the interest payments, let alone repay the capital sum. Often the solution is seen as easier bankruptcy laws and debt relief. Most people realise the incentive effects of these sometimes laudable actions – they increase the incentive to enter into debt and then to default, and as a result the price of credit will rise and many types of borrowers will be refused future loans. It is these effects and their control which are the focus of the economist's incentive analysis. As the late Arthur Leff, in prose designed to pull at our heartstrings, points out, while the economist's prescriptions may be harsh they are nonetheless true:

> There is an old widow, see, with six children. It is December and the weather is rotten. She defaults on the mortgage on her (and the babies') family home. The mortgagee, twirling his black moustache, takes the requisite legal steps to foreclose the mortgage and throw them all out into the cold. She pleads her total poverty to the judge. Rising behind the bench, the judge points her and her brood out into the swirling blizzard. 'Go', he says. 'Your plight moves me not'. 'How awful', you say?
>
> 'Nonsense', says the economi[st]. ... 'Look at the other side of the ... coin. What would happen if the judge let the

old lady stay on just because she was out of money? First of all, lenders would in the future be loath to lend to old widows with children. I don't say they wouldn't lend at all, they'd just be more careful about marginal cases, and raise the price of credit for the less marginal cases. The aggregate cost to the class of old ladies with homesteads would most likely rise more than the cost imposed on this particular widow. That is, the aggregate value of all their homes (known as their wealth) would fall, and they'd all be worse off.

'More than that, look at what such a decision would do to the motivation of old widows. Knowing that their failure to pay their debts would not be visited with swift retribution, they would have less incentive to prevent defaults. They might start giving an occasional piece of chicken to the kids, or even work up a fragment of beef from time to time. Profligacy like that would lead to even less credit-worthiness as their default rates climb. More and more of them would be priced out of the money market until no widow could ever *decide for herself* to mortgage her house to get the capital necessary to start a seamstress business to pull herself (and her infants) out of poverty. What do you mean, "awful"? What have you got against widows and orphans?'[2]

Assumption of economic rationality

What underpins the economist's incentive analysis is the premise that people, on average, behave in a rational, self-interested way. Or as the late George Stigler has said, economics is 'a stupendous palace erected on the granite of self-interest'.[3]

---

2   A. A. Leff, 'Economic analysis of law: some realism about nominalism', *Virginia Law Review*, 1974, 60: 460–61.

3   G. J. Stigler, *The Economist as Preacher*, Blackwell, Oxford, 1989, p. 136.

The economist's assumption of rationality or self-interest means no more than that people act purposively in pursuit of their self-chosen ends. Or simply that people prefer more to less of the things they desire.

The assumption that people act rationally has been much maligned and ridiculed. It is argued that people are not rational, that they cannot and do not calculate, and that rationality imputes a degree of computational skill and knowledge that not even economists possess. Veblen's brutal parody of economic man is a classic statement of this class of criticism: '… a lightning calculator of pleasures and pains, who oscillates like a homogeneous globule of … happiness under the impulse of stimuli that shift him about the area, but leave him intact'.[4]

Or Professor Kenneth Boulding's cutting dissection of 'economic man':

> It is a wonder indeed that economic institutions can survive
> at all, when economic man is so universally unpopular.
> No one in his senses would want his daughter to marry
> an economic man, one who counted every cost and asked
> for every reward, was never afflicted with mad generosity
> or uncalculating love, and who never acted out of a sense
> of inner identity, and indeed had no inner identity even
> if he was occasionally affected by carefully calculated
> considerations of benevolence or malevolence. The attack
> on economics is an attack on calculatedness, and the very
> fact that we think of calculating as cold, suggests how
> exposed economists are to romantic and heroic criticism.[5]

---

4   T. Veblen, 'Why is economics not an evolutionary science?' (1898), in *The Place of Science in Modern Civilization*, New York, 1919, p. 73.

5   K. E. Boulding, 'Economics as a moral science', *American Economic Review*, 1968, 58: 10.

These criticisms are caricatures that disguise more sophistic-ated ways of looking at this assumption. I will suggest several.

Box 2 Did economics create humans?

Since Adam Smith, economists have advocated free trade and the division of labour. Not even they claim, however, that such efficient behaviour created men and women. Yet recent research suggests that that the very existence of humans is due to economics. Horan, Bulte and Shogren[6] have purportedly shown that *Homo sapiens* (humans) displaced Neanderthal man and others because they engaged in trade and specialisation. The usual explanation for the extinction of Neanderthal man was that he was a stupid, hairy caveman outwitted by cleverer humans. Yet the evidence shows that Neanderthals lived successfully for 200,000 years before humans arrived in Europe, and that they engaged in the same hunting and food-gathering activities. One theory is that *Homo sapiens* had better tools; another that he could think symbolically and therefore cooperate and organise better. But Horan et al. argue that it was because he had a better economic system. Humans traded, and practised division of labour, while Neanderthals did not. A computer model that assumed that the two were similar in all respects except for humans' ability to trade and specialise – the most efficient hunters hunted, while bad hunters made clothes and tools, and both then traded with one another – showed that humans outbred and outhunted cavemen. According to the model, humans were able to get more meat, which drove up their

---

6   R. D. Horan, E. Bulte and J. F. Shogren, 'How trade saved humanity from biolo-gical exclusion: an economic theory of Neanderthal extinction', *Journal of Economic Behavior and Organization*, 2005, 58: 1–29.

fertility and increased their population. Given a finite amount of meat, this left less for the Neanderthals, and their population went into decline. What is fascinating about the research is how fast Neanderthals become extinct – depending on the numbers, it's between 2,500 and 30,000 years, a range that conforms to the evidence. Thus humans are what they are today, it seems, because they are economic man or *Homo economicus*.

If people do not behave in predictable ways, then the idea that we can regulate society by laws and incentives becomes untenable. Yet the whole basis of business, law and social activity is the assumption that people on average do respond in predictable ways. We know, for example, that when the price of a certain make of car increases relative to others, fewer of those cars are bought. The assumption of rationality is used by economists not as a description of all human behaviour but as a way of identifying the predictable component of the response of the average individual in a group. This use of the rationality assumption conceives of economic man as a weighted average of the group of individuals under investigation. It thus allows for marked differences in individual responses.

The second way of looking at the assumption of rationality is to ask what model of man we regard as the most appropriate for framing laws. Can we safely assume that all men are good citizens and altruistic, or should we guard against the worst possible outcome by assuming that men are selfish and seek to maximise only their own welfare? Some legal and political theorists have argued that the latter assumption should be employed. Oliver

Wendell Holmes argued that: 'If you want to know the law and nothing else, you must look at it as a bad man, who cares only for the material consequences which such knowledge enables him to predict, not as a good one, who finds his reasons for conduct, whether inside the law or outside of it, in the vaguer sanctions of the conscience.'[7]

What Holmes is saying here (in my view) is not that all men are bad, or that men obey the law only because they fear the consequences, but that this is a prudent model of man upon which to frame laws. Thus one can consistently hold the view that man is by nature law-abiding but that the best model to base our laws on is one in which 'bad men' are constrained. This idea goes back even farther, to the seventeenth-century political philosopher Thomas Hobbes, who said in *Leviathan* (1651): 'In constraining any system of government, and fixing the several checks and controls on the constitution, every man ought to be supposed a knave, and to have no other end, in all his actions, than private interest.'

Economists do it with models

Another major difference, and a cause of tension between lawyer and economist, concerns the role of theory. As Patrick Atiyah has observed:

Most English judges are emphatically neither intellectuals nor theorists; few are ever given to doubting their own first principles, at least in public, and most are deeply sceptical of the value of theory ... Very few have more than the faintest glimmering of the vast jurisprudential literature

---

7   O. W. Holmes, 'The path of the law', *Harvard Law Review*, 1897, 10: 478.

concerning the nature *of* the judicial process. Most would pride themselves on being pragmatists, and not theorists.[8]

Lawyers do not think in terms of theories. The lawyer's method of analysis is literary; it is reasoning by metaphor, analogy and simile. His empirical method is the study of past cases and statutes, common sense, introspection, anecdotes and experience. Indeed, the common-law method, which has had a profound effect on legal thinking, is intensely pragmatic and inductive. It is, as Judge Bork has said, 'a ship with a great deal of sail but a very shallow keel'.[9]

Moreover, lawyers are hostile to theory with its broad generalisations based on simplifying assumptions. The law, argues the lawyer, will not yield to a single theory – it is too complex and confused; and rides many different horses at the same time. The postulates of the economist seem to the lawyer fragile, narrow and technical, and to be couched in so many qualifications as to render the economist's pronouncements irrelevant; or they are stated with such sweeping generality that it is difficult to apply them to specific factual settings. Lawyers are more prone to consider simultaneously all the facts, and to evaluate propositions with reference to specific individuals. The economist will argue that people are deterred by higher-damage awards from acting negligently, all other things being constant. The lawyer will counter with the claim that Mrs M., the defendant in the case, would not have taken more care because she did not think about the law or was

8   P. S. Atiyah, 'The legacy of Holmes through English eyes', *Boston University Law Review*, 1983, 63: 380.

9   R. H. Bork, 'New constitutional theories threaten rights, Bork warns', AEI Memorandum no. 44, American Enterprise Institute, Washington, DC, 1985, p. 8.

not even aware of it at the time. The economist will counter that one does not have to show that *every* individual will be deterred, only that, on average, individuals will be, and, moreover, that particular instances do not refute the theory because the evidence that could conceivably support the proposition would not come to the attention of lawyers – that is, a lower caseload and fewer people acting negligently.

Lawyers too often regard their task as similar to that of the judge. They analyse the law using the same language, reasoning and categories as judges and, therefore, are trapped into seeing the law in the same narrow way. When applied to developing a theoretical framework for the law this is doomed to failure, since it inevitably gives the same answers and the same reasons as judges do. This approach will never reveal startling insights nor cut through the complexity and confusion of reality.

At the root of the lawyer's criticism is a confusion of theory with description. Economists, on the other hand, adopt a scientific approach. They think in terms of models and use simplifying assumptions to make complex problems manageable. These models are often criticised as being unrealistic and simplistic. Of course they are! What possible benefit could there be in recreating reality in a more formal way? The answer must be none. A model's value is the way it sheds new insights on what were before confused and complicated matters, to reveal the connections between disparate areas and to unearth the 'common ground'.

Models are based on assumptions, and assumptions by their nature are unrealistic. Here we must pause to consider the nature of theory, especially positive theory. Positive economic theory is a set of generalisations used to predict the consequences of change. There is one school of thought in economics, led by Milton Friedman, which claims that it is never legitimate to criticise a theory because its assumptions are unrealistic. The only way to evaluate a theory is to see whether its predictions, by which we mean its postulated relationships, are supported by empirical evidence. Moreover, where two theories are equally capable of explaining the same observations, the simpler is to be preferred. This is because theory and science seek generality. The more assumptions that are employed and the more specific the theory, the less general it will become and the less it will explain.

In short, *theory must be simple and unrealistic.* Its value lies in revealing connections hitherto unknown and in giving its possessor a compass to guide him through the (mostly irrelevant) complexity of the real world. As Milton Friedman has stated: 'A fundamental hypothesis of science is that appearances are deceptive and that there is a way of looking at or interpreting or organizing the evidence that will reveal superficially disconnected and diverse phenomena to be manifestations of a more fundamental and relatively simple structure.'[10]

Positive versus normative economics

Economists work with different types of theory. The most common distinction is between positive economics (what is) and normative economics (what ought to be).

Positive theories seek to explain observed outcomes, and to predict behaviour. Their validity – whether they are a successful or good theory – must be assessed by the evidence that has been

---

10 M. Friedman, 'The methodology of positive economics', in *Essays in Positive Economics*, University of Chicago Press, Chicago, 1953, p. 33.

amassed in support of the predictions and explanations. That is, positive economics is the empirical branch of economics. The economics of crime is a good example of this use of economics (see Chapter 5).

Normative, or welfare, economics is the ethical branch of economics. It seeks to rank outcomes and policies in terms of good and bad based on stated ethical norms or welfare criteria. The most commonly used approach is economic efficiency, which evaluates laws and policies using the efficiency or the wealth maximisation norm. There is, however, a vast literature using other distributive and *ex ante* norms and concepts of justice.

Empirical analysis

Bob Cooter has remarked: 'Left to its own devices, the law stood no more chance of developing quantitative methodology than Australia stood of developing the rabbit.'[11] Economists, on the other hand, thrive on quantitative study, and have at their disposal many sophisticated statistical techniques that can be used to quantify the impact of the law. Although not all legal questions are amenable to statistical analysis, those which are can be examined with more rigour and statistical validity (in the context of an explicitly formulated theory) through the use of economics. Economists have occupied this niche with great vigour. More

---

11 R. D. Cooter, 'Law and the imperialism of economics: an introduction to the economic analysis of law and a review of the major books', *UCLA Law Review*, 1982, 29: 1260.

recently econometric and statistical testing[12] of economic theory has been introduced in regulatory and court proceedings in Europe in the areas of competition law, regulation of utilities and in the estimation of damages. Economists have also broadened their toolkit of empirical analysis to case studies, surveys, simulations and experimental techniques.

Law without ethics[13]

Economic analysis of law has been called 'dehumanising', a 'mechanical, hedonistic analysis of legal relationships'. The practitioners of the aptly named 'dismal science' want to sell babies,[14] body parts, blood,[15] and to 'commodify' everything, thereby debasing all human activities and treating law in crude managerial terms, say the critics.

These criticisms are in large part an inevitable consequence of an approach that emphasises trade-offs (the principle of substitution at the margin), is instrumental (relates ends to their means of attainment), and which seeks to make explicit choices that are implicit and go unrecognised. In practice, it is astounding how rarely lawyers and civil servants are prepared to state clearly the goal of a law or to assess the extent to which specific laws have

---

12 F. M. Fisher, 'Multiple regression in legal proceedings', *Columbia Law Review*, 1980, 80: 702–36; D. L. Rubinfeld, 'Econometrics in the courtroom', *Columbia Law Review*, 1985, 85: 1040–92.

13 The phrase is borrowed from Gordon Tullock's subtitle to *The Logic of the Law*, Basic Books, New York, 1970.

14 E. M. Landes and R. A. Posner, 'The economics of the baby shortage', *Journal of Legal Studies*, 1978, 7: 323–48. Cf. J. R. S. Prichard, 'A market for babies', *University of Toronto Law Journal*, 1984, 34: 341–57.

15 R. Kessel, 'Transfused blood, serum hepatitis, and the Coase Theorem', *Journal of Law and Economics*, 1974, 17: 265–89.

achieved their intended results. The approach is usually in terms of definitions, procedures and wording, rather than costs, benefits and results. Ask any lawyer or civil servant what evidence exists or research has been undertaken on the effects of the criminal laws, policing or health and safety legislation: How much has it cost? How many lives/crimes have been saved/prevented? Is it effective? – questions that receive only quizzical looks and a collective shrug of the shoulders.

It is precisely these questions which economics addresses and which alienate lawyers and lawmakers. But while lawyers and policy-makers can reject the economist's answers, they cannot ignore them. Every law, indeed every moral question, involves a choice, entails a trade-off and hence gives rise to a cost. Economists make the conditions of these legal and moral choices explicit.

Economists do sometimes have a problem of communication. Their treatment of law appears strained because it uses the metaphors and prose of the marketplace. Many articles applying economics to law model by analogy with the market. For example, the economist will talk about the 'supply of and demand for' crime, the penalty as a 'price' to engage in crime, thereby conveying the impression that he believes that if criminals are willing to 'pay' an appropriate 'price' they can rape and pillage at will.

Two comments are apposite. First, economists should not be taken too literally. They, like other professionals and 'experts', have fallen victim to jargon and acronym. The language of market analysis is frequently used to organise analysis, as shorthand to distinguish the main factors relevant to the economic appraisal of a particular issue. But it is not the claim of economists that a 'market', say, in crime exists or should exist, only that there is a 'supply' of criminal offences and a desire on the part of the prospective victims and society to prevent those crimes.

Second, it is also true that economic metaphors are deeply embedded in the moral language used to describe crime and punishment: 'pay the price for his misdeeds', 'reap his rewards', 'the wages of sin', 'pay his debt to society', and so on. Also, the predominant sanction of the common law is financial damages, while the fine is the cornerstone of the Anglo-American penal system. These sanctions can be viewed as a penalty or, alternatively, as a price for engaging in an illegal activity, just as the price of a loaf of bread can be viewed as measuring its value, giving producers a reward and incentive to produce bread, penalising the consumer who buys bread for making a call on society's scarce resources and deterring those from consuming bread who do not value it very highly or cannot afford it. Just because something is called a price, a penalty or a civil or criminal sanction should not seduce us into thinking that the different labels necessarily carry analytical and behavioural differences.

Sometimes it is suggested that what really separates lawyers and economists is justice. Economists are interested in economic efficiency; lawyers in justice. This distinction has some truth, but turns out on closer examination to be largely semantic.

The *Concise Oxford Dictionary* defines justice as 'fairness; exercise of authority in maintenance of a right'. Thus, when it is claimed that the law seeks justice, all that is being contended is that the authority of the law is being exercised to protect and enforce the rights defined by law. This is circular. The word 'justice' has no ethical content when used in this way. It tells us nothing of the value or morality of specific legal rights. As Steven Lucas states in *On Justice*: 'the formal idea of equality or justice as a lodestar of social policy is devoid of all meaning; it is possible to advance every kind of postulate in the name of justice'.[16]

Summing up

At the core of economics is the assumption that individuals act purposively to select those alternatives in those quantities which maximise their welfare as perceived by them. It is this assumption which gives economics its explanatory power – the ability to anticipate better than other approaches the consequences of changes in the conditions of choice.

The theory of choice, which underpins economics, leads to a fundamentally different view of law which, while not alien to lawyers, is not central. As I have argued, economists perceive the law as a giant pricing machine which conveys incentives and affects actions and outcomes. Its framework of duties, rights and obligations creates a system of constraints and penalties that alter the net benefits of different courses of action. In a crude way, the law prices and taxes individual human behaviour and therefore influences that behaviour.

---

16   S. Lucas, *On Justice*, Clarendon Press, Oxford, 1989, p. 31.

4 THE ECONOMIC APPROACH

Economics is typically viewed as the study of inflation, unemployment and markets, subjects that seem to have only a glancing relevance to whether a negligent doctor should compensate his patient for sawing off the wrong leg, whether a newspaper should pay compensation in a libel action, or what types of safety regulation are effective. Yet the economic analysis of law uses the same economics to investigate these questions as it does to analyse the price of timber. This is known as price theory: the study of the interaction and behaviour of individual units in the economy – the firm, the consumer and the worker.

A biblical parable

The question naturally arises as to why economics has any role to play in legal analysis and the law. Perhaps the best way to see the intimate relationship between law and economics is to consider the following biblical parable.

When God created the world he put Adam and Eve in the Garden of Eden. At more or less the same time he did two other things:

- *first*, he laid down a 'law': don't eat the apples;
- *second*, he gave Adam and Eve the ability to choose.

We all know what they did. They broke the law and committed the human race to eternal damnation in a world where resources are scarce and where people are selfish. God gave man a choice – a legal choice – and man created an economic problem. Instead of basking in an effortless paradise he is required to toil and to determine his own destiny. Thus our legal and economic systems began with the same act of law-breaking.

This biblical parable offers us several truths. First, that law and economics deal with essentially the same problems: scarcity with its conflict of interests and how to channel selfishness into socially desirable outcomes. Economists and lawyers may not belong to the oldest profession, although they are frequently accused of behaving as if they did, but they are both concerned with resolving the oldest problem – how to reconcile individual freedoms when individual interests conflict. The market is one solution; the law another. And the two interact.

Second, economists have been wise to build their discipline on a model of man which assumes that he acts principally out of self-interest. On the whole, people are not saints. A legal or economic system that is built on altruism would soon collapse, even if it offers people the prospect of paradise. God could not do it; no man or society has yet proved God deficient.

Finally, it tells us that, even with the assistance of divine guidance, it is a mistake to believe that there is a one-to-one correspondence between what the law says and what people do. People will obey the law only if it is in their interests to do so, and they will, in any event, try to minimise the disadvantages that laws impose on them.

Economics – choice and scarcity

Economics, then, is about scarcity and the choices that the Adams and Eves of this world make. It is the systematic study of choice under conditions of scarcity: the advantages and disadvantages and the way these are balanced, and the way individuals evolve social institutions to deal with scarcity and to control private interest.

The view of many contemporary economists, and the one that lies at the root of the extension of economics to law, is that any question which involves a choice, whether it be the price to be charged by a gas utility or the determination of liability by a judge, has an economic dimension. It is concerned with analysing the choices that individuals in their roles as judges, people at risk, litigants and lawyers make in response to harms, to the law and to other factors such as costs, income and so on.

Costs and benefits

Whether we like it or not, or whether we approve of economics or not, economic considerations do have a profound effect on the way the law functions in practice. Take the example of tort, which, as will be shown below, governs civil liability for wrongs such as negligently caused motor accidents. Accidents and harms are not only physical events giving rise to the possibility of legal action and medical treatment; they are also economic events. An accident consumes resources; its avoidance is costly, and the hospitalisation and medical treatment of victims are also costly. In a society where resources are scarce, rules of law are required that provide not only a just solution but one that avoids waste by reducing the costs of accidents.

Economics places at the forefront of discussion the costs and benefits of the law, considerations that will always be relevant when resources are limited. All too often, lawyers (politicians, pressure groups and civil servants) discuss the law as if it were costless. Economics informs us that nothing is free from the viewpoint of society as a whole. Increasing access to the courts, for example, consumes resources that will not then be available for other uses. As Leff succinctly puts it: 'the central tenet and most important operative principle of economic analysis is to ask of every move (1) how much will it cost?; (2) who pays?; and (3) who ought to decide both questions?'[1]

Efficiency defined

The economist brings together his concern for costs, benefits and incentive effects in the concept of economic efficiency or wealth maximisation. There are two versions of economic efficiency typically used:

- **Pareto efficiency**, where the joint gains from trade are exploited so that the parties cannot be made better off; and

- **Kaldor-Hicks efficiency**, or wealth maximisation or the cost–benefit test, which measures economic welfare in terms of the maximisation of the difference between economic benefits and economic costs.

The efficiency principle can be used in at least two ways – as the basis for generating predictions (positive or explanatory theory), and as a normative framework to assess good and bad, or

---

1   Leff, 'Economic analysis of law', op. cit., p. 460.

better and worse. The former is best illustrated by the economics of crime (Chapter 5), and the latter by economic assessments of legal reform or the more contentious use of economics to provide an ethical basis for laws.

Willingness to pay

In order to evaluate an activity that produces a variety of benefits we must have some common measuring rod. Economists use money. But we must be clear not to confuse the way economists measure benefits with the purely financial aspects of a problem. The economic benefits are measured by the 'willingness-to-pay' of those individuals who are affected. That is, the economist's notion of benefit is similar to the utilitarian notion of happiness, but it is happiness backed by willingness-to-pay. Mere desire or 'need' is not relevant. The willingness-to-pay measure seeks to provide a quantitative indication of an individual's *intensity* of preferences.

Consider two examples where the measures of financial and economic benefit differ.

In many markets identical goods frequently sell for the same price to all customers. It follows that individuals with an intense preference for the good (i.e. who would be prepared to pay more) are receiving a substantial benefit from their purchase which is not measured in the market. Moreover, this surplus benefit is not captured as additional profit to the manufacturer. The economist calls this benefit *consumers' surplus* – the difference between the maximum sum an individual would be willing to pay and the sum he actually pays. It is the counterpart for the consumer of economic profit to the firm. The goal of an efficient economic system is to maximise the joint surplus of consumers and manufacturers, not the market price or money profits.

Economists appreciate that decisions are made on the basis of both monetary and non-monetary attributes. Take, for example, the choice of a job. An individual does not accept a job solely on the basis of its wage or salary, but of the whole package of benefits that go with it – the fringe benefits, working conditions, prospects of advancement, security of employment, travel, the reputation of the firm or institution, its location, and so on. As a result, people are willing to trade money for more of these attractive factors. Thus academic lawyers are paid substantially less than practising solicitors, and presumably they remain academics because the total non-monetary benefits exceed the higher salary they could earn in practice. Looked at another way, they are paying for the privilege of consuming these benefits in terms of the forgone salary.

The economist deals with this situation by measuring the non-monetary benefits in terms of the money that the individual gives up. That is, there is a 'monetary equivalent' of these benefits which, when added to the pecuniary salary, gives us the money value of the total package of benefits received from employment in a particular job. This is done not because the money itself is valuable – in fact it has no intrinsic value for an economist – but because it provides a simple means of comparing diverse attributes and alternatives.

Valuing intangibles

It is frequently argued that many aspects of life cannot be reduced to a monetary value – the so-called intangibles of freedom, life, love and the environment. It would be fruitless to deny that these are non-economic in character and often not traded in the market. But it would be equally foolish to suppose that the point undermines economic analysis. Many intangibles can be valued in monetary terms, and implicitly are so valued by individuals and society daily, and often the value attached to these non-pecuniary factors – such as the environment, traffic congestion, quality of life and other amenities – can be measured.[2]

Take the example of personal safety. It is often said that life is priceless, that it does not have a monetary value, and that any attempt to give it one is evil. Two observations should be made.

First, if life is regarded as priceless by individuals and society, we would never observe people taking any action involving personal risk. Something that has an infinite value must be preserved at any cost! But we, and the people around us, take risks every day, some quite substantial. The plain fact is that the actions of individuals imply that they do not regard their life as priceless, and are willing to trade the *risk* of death for material and psychic benefits.

Second, our social institutions do 'price' life. In tort we do not kill the person who negligently takes the life of another; we require only that he/she pays compensation. Look at it in a slightly different way: the law is in effect saying that you can kill a person through negligence so long as you are willing to pay the 'price'. If society really did regard life as 'priceless', would it adopt such a lax response – as it does in courtrooms every day – to situations where it is believed that the individual could have prevented a fatal accident if only more care had been taken?

The economics of safety provides a good illustration of the way economists link monetary valuation to resource allocation. The benefits of safety efforts are measured primarily in terms of

---

2   R. B. Palmquist and V. Kerry Smith, 'The use of property value techniques for policy and litigation', *International Yearbook of Environmental and Resource Economics*, vol. VI, Edward Elgar, Cheltenham, 2002, pp. 115–64.

the willingness to pay of those individuals at risk to reduce the accident rate. The economist does not ask the question: how much would you pay to stay alive? He asks the more subtle question: how much are you willing to pay to reduce the risk of death given that you do not know when, and if, you will be killed? That is, the amount of money the individual is willing to pay to reduce the *risk* of death or put more prosaically to save a 'statistical life'.

The economist's willingness-to-pay approach can be explained as follows. You cross a dangerously busy road each morning. You can cross it in one of two ways – by using a pedestrian crossing, which adds five minutes to your travel time, or by waiting for a gap in the traffic and rushing across. The latter action increases the likelihood of you being killed by one in a million – a small risk by all accounts. If you valued your own life at an infinite amount you would not take the risk, or, indeed, *any* risks. This is because you would be comparing an infinite loss against a finite cost of taking greater care. But we observe people taking these risks every day and some dying as a result. What are we to make of such actions? It is this. People, in deciding what care they will take, gauge the costs of greater precautions against the risks, and are willing to trade improvements in their material welfare for decreases or increases in risks. A pedestrian's decision not to use a crossing implicitly trades time for risk. *Ex ante*, this trade seems reasonable and from it we can derive the value that the group taking such action places on a statistical death.

Let me illustrate how one would make such a calculation. Suppose the saving in time to each person from not using the pedestrian crossing is 60 pence and the increase in risk is one in a million. The decision not to use the crossing implies a value of at least £600,000 (= 60 pence multiplied by 1 million). Put differently, the value of a pedestrian crossing that saves one statistical life is £600,000. It is, therefore, economically worthwhile to spend up to £600,000 to construct such a crossing.

This approach was controversially brought to light by John Graham (subsequently appointed head of the US Office of Management and Budget) when in 2001 he claimed US health and environmental rules had caused the 'statistical murder' of 60,000 people every year through the inefficient allocation of funds owing to regulatory requirements.[3] One example he gave was that in the USA: 'We regulate potentially carcinogenic benzene emissions during waste operations at a cost of US$19 million per year of life saved, while 70 percent of women over the age of fifty do not receive regular mammograms, an intervention that costs roughly US$17,000 per year of life saved.' His point was that a reallocation of effort and resources would lead to more life saved – inefficient regulation kills!

A more general principle can be derived from the economics of safety, and any other tangible or intangible activity. It is an answer to, or at least some guidance on, the vexing question of 'How safe is safe?' and, in the case of tort law, discussed later, 'What is reasonable care?'

There exists an optimal amount of safety defined by the costs and benefits of risk reduction. Many risks (accidents) can be reduced by taking more care, but only at a higher cost. The economic problem is to locate the point where the marginal costs of more safety are balanced by the marginal reduction in expected accident losses. Optimal care is achieved when an additional pound, dollar or euro is spent on reducing risks which saves one

---

3   T. Tengs et al., 'Five hundred life saving interventions and their cost-effectiveness', *Risk Analysis*, 1995, 15: 369–90.

pound, dollar or euro in *expected* accident losses. Optimal defined in this way means that many accidents are 'justified' because they would be too costly to avoid. The corollary to this is that, just as there can be too little care and safety, there can also be excessive amounts. By framing the question in terms of resource allocation, the economist is able to adopt a consistent valuation procedure to allocate scarce resources to saving lives.

Opportunity costs

It is widely believed that economists are obsessed with financial costs and benefits to the exclusion of all else. This is not the case. Accountants deal with financial costs and profits, not economists. Economists are concerned with choice and resource allocation, and their definition of cost is radically *subjective* and intimately related to individual choices operating within the forces of demand and supply. This is why a theory that predicts people's reactions to changes in the factors affecting benefits and costs is so central to economics. Without the ability to anticipate the way consumers and suppliers will react to changes, it would not be possible to quantify the gains and losses of laws and regulations.

The economic cost of a thing is its value in the next-best, forgone alternative use. Economists cost things in this way because they are concerned with the way resources are allocated, and want to ensure that resources are allocated to their highest-valued uses. It is important not to confuse accounting or historical costs with economic costs. If you bought a house for £100,000 six years ago and are now offered £300,000, the cost of the house is £300,000, not £100,000. It is £300,000 because that is what you are now giving up to remain in the house and is the house's next-best alternative use.

If I produce a good, the costs of production not only reflect my outlay on labour, plant and materials but the profit I sacrifice in not using those resources in their next-best use. It follows that the notion of economic profit makes an allowance for a 'normal' rate of return on capital (for example, what you could earn by keeping the money in a safe bank account). It therefore should not be confused with profits as measured by the accountants. Clearly, if the next-best use of my resources is more profitable than their current use, then I am earning economic losses, not profits – even though I am showing an accounting profit. The prudent investor would realise this, and reallocate his or her activities to their highest-valued uses. This is why economists assert, paradoxically, that under perfect competition firms earn no excess 'economic' profits.

Coasian economics

The concept of opportunity costs just explained is the bedrock of the Coase Theorem and the economics of law.

The Coase Theorem

The Coase Theorem states that in the absence of transactions costs the legal position does not affect the efficiency with which resources are allocated.[4] It can be illustrated by taking the facts in the 1879 case of *Sturges v Bridgman* discussed by Coase. A confectioner in Wigmore Street used two mortars and pestles, one being in operation in the same position for over 60 years. This caused

---

4   This simplifies Coase's analysis and the effects of different liability laws. See C. G. Veljanovski, 'The Coase Theorems and the economic theory of markets and law', *Kyklos*, 1982, 35: 53–74.

his neighbour – a doctor – no bother for eight years until he built a consulting room at the end of his garden right next to the confectioner's kitchen. The noise and vibration made it difficult for the doctor to use the consulting room. The doctor sued the confectioner, claiming that the noise was excessive.

Will what the court decides affect the use of these two plots of land? Coase's answer was 'no', provided the doctor and confectioner can negotiate.

To establish this we need to assign monetary values to the gains and losses of both parties. Assume that the profit from making confectionery is £400 and that the loss of profit inflicted on the doctor is £300. The efficient solution is for the confectioner to continue using his machinery (a gain of £400 minus £300 = £100).

Suppose that the court decides, in flagrant disregard of these economic facts, to award the doctor an injunction that requires the confectioner to cease the noise. You may think that this will freeze the land in an inefficient use. But you would be wrong. If the court, as it did, awards the injunction, the confectioner has an incentive to bargain with the doctor to, in effect, 'buy out' the injunction. In terms of the figures that have been assigned, the doctor values peace and quiet only at £300, whereas the confectioner values productive noise at £400. A mutually advantageous bargain can be struck between them – the confectioner would be willing to pay the doctor up to £400 for something the doctor values at only £300. There is thus a bargaining range of £100 where some agreement can be reached, although the exact payment cannot be predicted since it depends on the bargaining abilities of the parties. The injunction forms only the starting point for negotiation; it does not influence the pattern of land use.

If the case had been decided the other way, the judicially imposed solution would be the final solution and it would, on the figures assumed, be the efficient solution. Since the doctor has not got his injunction he must, if he wants less noise, bargain with the confectioner. But, since his loss is only £300 and the confectioner's profit is £400, he cannot offer the confectioner a sum sufficient to induce him to stop using his mortars and pestles.

From this example we can see that two totally opposite legal rules lead to the same outcome. Further, in both cases the confectioner 'bears' the loss – when he is liable he bears the loss in the sum he pays the doctor; when he is not the loss he inflicts on the doctor is taken into account by the payment he refuses to take from the doctor to stop making noise. The latter is an opportunity cost of his business because he could readily convert his legal right into cash. As Coase states, in economics 'the receipt forgone of a given amount is the equivalent of a payment of the same amount'.

Implications of opportunity cost analysis

Coase's analysis of the problem of social costs generates a number of important economic propositions and insights.

First, the economist's cost–benefit analysis or efficiency criterion is not confined to financial costs and accounting profits, but has a much wider ambit. It has to do with choice, with the balancing of competing claims on scarce resources. A lawyer would call this balancing the interests of the plaintiff and the defendant. But these different ways of expressing the problem recognise that, if we make a decision in favour of one party, we harm the other. The question is: on what basis do we make the decision having regard to the parties' interests and rights? The economist offers a technical algorithm: evaluate all the advantages and disadvantages to both parties in money terms and minimise the sum of the joint costs – or, which is the same, the parties' joint wealth.

Second, Coase subtly undermined the notion that the physical causation of harm is key to the economics of market failure, and that this is recognised by the common law. The claim 'A hurt B' was hitherto sufficient in economics to attribute the costs of harmful activities to the entity causing them. Coase showed that this was incorrect. The harm results from the proximity of two incompatible activities – remove one and the harm disappears. Losses are therefore the result of the interaction of two incompatible or interfering activities and are properly to be treated as the *joint cost* of both activities. This line of reasoning suggests that all victims are partly the 'authors' of their own misfortune. In the allocative sense this is correct. In terms of the legal choice that has to be made, the 'harm' is reciprocal in character: to permit the defendant to continue is to harm the plaintiff; to decide in favour of the plaintiff inflicts harm on the defendant. The economist uses the word 'costs' where the lawyer would use 'interests'. But that should not mislead us. The economist's balancing of costs and benefits is no different from the judgmental process engaged in by the courts in resolving most legal disputes.

Third, the Coase Theorem indicates that the law has no allocative effect if transactions costs are negligible. In practice, where transactions costs are low it can be expected that bargaining around the law will minimise its impact. Coase's analysis points to the need to go beyond the law. When transactions costs are low the parties will be able to bargain around the law, adjusting their relationships and contracts to offset any reallocation of costs and liabilities. Thus laws that make employers liable for injuries to their workers might not increase the costs to employers because wages might fall to offset damage payments. Likewise, making manufacturers liable for defective products might simply increase the price of goods without any improvement in safety or in consumer welfare. The lesson for lawyers is that individuals react to laws in ways that minimise the burdens those laws place upon them.

Fourth, Coase's analysis emphasises the critical importance of transactions costs as a principal determinant of the law's effects on economic activity and behaviour. It is no exaggeration to say that the intellectual bridge between law and economics has, as one of its main supporting arches, the notion of transactions costs. Transactions costs can be defined as the costs of information and bargaining, and of defining, policing and enforcing property rights and contracts. In short, they are the frictions associated with transacting. Transactions costs have two effects, which can be termed a static and a dynamic effect. First, they block otherwise wealth-maximising market transactions. In *Sturges v Bridgman* they would have fixed land in inefficient uses if the judge had decided incorrectly. If transactions costs are sufficiently high the law will have economic effects and the investigator must turn to an identification of the source and size of transactions costs properly to analyse the law and possible reform. Second, Coase suggested that many institutions – among them the firm, commodity exchange and contract – can be explained as efficient adaptations to transactions costs.

Fifth, the economic function of law is not to prevent all harm but to minimise costs or maximise benefits. Only rarely will economic considerations lead to such extreme solutions as the complete elimination of pollution or accidents, even if such radical solutions were technically feasible. As the judge in *Daborn v Bath Tramways*[5] observed: 'As has been pointed out, if all the trains in this country were restricted to a speed of five miles an hour, there would be fewer accidents, but our national life would be intolerably slowed down.'

The economic approach often means not an either/or solution characteristic of legal outcomes, but a positive level of harm based on the incremental costs of avoiding the loss balanced against the incremental losses that have been prevented. When these joint costs cannot be further reduced we have the 'efficient' or 'optimal' level of harm.

---

5   [1946] 2 All ER 333.

5 SOME LEGAL APPLICATIONS

It is now time to put some flesh on the economics of law by discussing several specific applications.

The roles of the economist

The economic analysis of law involves three distinct but related efforts – the use of economics to determine the effects of law, to identify economically efficient law, and to predict or explain legal rules and remedies. The economist Alvin Klevorick has recast these into the different roles that economists can play in legal analysis:[1]

- **Technician** – the economist can accept the legal problem as formulated by lawyers and seek to solve it by applying economics. Company A breaches its contract with B for the supply of machinery resulting in lost profits to B: what is the correct basis on which to calculate the lost profits? In UK and European competition laws the definition of the 'relevant market' and competitive assessments require the skills of an economist to identify barriers to entry, the degree of cross-elasticity between similar products which would class

---

1 These categories are taken from A. Klevorick, 'Law and economic theory: an economist's view', *American Economic Review*, 1975, 65: 237–43.

them as economic substitutes, and the extent of competition between sellers (see Chapter 4). Here the economist is assisting lawyers, regulators and judges to apply the law without in any way challenging their approach or authority. Below we look at how economics can assist in determining the amount that those who are injured should receive in compensation through the courts.

- **Supertechnician** – the second role is that of the *supertechnician.* Here the economist treats an area of law as if its objective were to improve the allocation of resources in the economy. A good example is the economics of crime. The use of economics to study crime was once ridiculed, but today it is now playing an important role in the formulation of policy. For example, the UK Home Office (similar to the US Department of Justice) recently advertised for economists under the heading 'What do crime, drugs and migration have to do with economics?' Its answer:

> The Home Office has a mission to build a safe, just and tolerant society. Such far-reaching and fundamental aims demand significant resources, and we command a budget of £18bn per year. … But with such ambitious objectives any amount of resources is going to be limited, which makes ensuring that Home Office policy is as effective and efficient as it can be of paramount importance.
>
> That's where you come in. As a Home Office Economic Advisor, you will be applying the latest economic thinking to understand the drivers of crime, applying modelling techniques to predict future crime levels and offending behaviour as well as assessing the performance of policies. You will use

your knowledge of markets to help determine the most effective interventions to combat drug use, organised crime and illegal immigration. Your understanding of organisations and market structure can be applied to contestability of services and devising the most effective relationships between the Home Office and its delivery agents. You will also apply sophisticated valuation techniques to measure the cost to society of criminal activity.[2]

- **Economic rhetorician** – the economist's third role is what may be termed that of *economic rhetorician.* This role employs economic concepts and terms to provide a new vocabulary for lawyers. It can take the form of a full-blown efficiency analysis such as Posner's hypothesis that the common law can be explained 'as if' judges are trying to bring about a more efficient allocation of resources. Alternatively, economic principles can be used to organise the decisions of judges – categorising them, drawing out the common threads, defining legal terms more clearly, and criticising them and the laws by pointing to inconsistencies in reasoning, and so on. In other words, the economist is here using economics to make general propositions about the law in a way lawyers would find intuitively acceptable.

Personal injury damages

Consider first the economist as a technician. Under English common law the object of the award of damages generally, and specifically to a negligently injured plaintiff, is to provide

---

2   *The Economist*, 9 April 2005.

'full compensation' in the sense of placing the person in the same position that he or she would have been in had the injury not occurred, in so far as money can. The economist, actuary and accountant can all assist the court in achieving the goal of full compensation defined in this way. Yet, surprisingly, until recently the English judiciary has discouraged expert evidence in personal injury and death cases, preferring a relatively unsophisticated arithmetical calculation which had the effect of severely under-compensating the victims of accidents until recently.

This has been the case for damages for future personal injury losses. Many accident victims suffer continuing losses which impair their ability to work full time or as productively as before the accident. In such cases the judge must estimate the future lost stream of income, and then discount this by some interest rate to arrive at a fixed sum to award the victim as 'full' compensation. Instead of using economic and actuarial evidence, the English courts use a *multiplier/multiplicand* approach. This has two parts. First, the judge determines the victim's annual loss arising from the accident. This is a question of fact. The court must then convert this annual sum into the present value of the plaintiff's prospective loss. The judge does this by first determining a multiplier which he uses to multiply the victim's annual loss. The implied multiplier takes into account two factors – discounting to reflect the time value of money, and an allowance for what lawyers refer to as the 'vicissitudes of life'. Discounting is required to adjust for the fact that the victim is in early receipt of his compensation and can invest it over the remaining period of his life to earn an annuity. The courts also adjust future losses downwards to take account of contingencies that would reduce the loss attributable to the accident, such as remarriage, the prospect of unemployment and the likelihood of illnesses that could shorten life. These factors are not explicitly taken into account in any principled arithmetic fashion. Rather, the judge (juries no longer sit in civil trials in England and Wales with the exception of libel actions) arrives at a figure that in his judgment provides 'full' compensation.

Before recent reforms of the law in this area, the courts used multipliers between 5 and 18, with 15 often the maximum. These were low, and led to severe under-compensation of injured victims. Indeed, most legal practitioners and judges remained ignorant of the discount rate implied by multipliers until Lord Diplock revealed in 1979 that it was around 4 to 5 per cent.[3] Kemp and others have argued both for the increased use of actuarial evidence and for a discount rate of around 1.5 to 2.3 per cent per annum.[4]

To illustrate the impact of the court's choice of multiplier (and implicitly the discount rate), consider the facts in *Mitchell* v. *Mulholland*[5] (incidentally a case in which Lord Justice Edmund Davies ruled that the expert evidence of economists was inadmissible). Using the 'multiplier' approach, the Court of Appeal multiplied the plaintiff's net pre-trial loss of annual earnings by 14 to arrive at total damages of £20,833.

If an economist had been asked to compensate the plaintiff in *Mitchell v Mulholland*, he would have ended up much better off.[6] Using the plaintiff's annual net earnings at the time of injury

---

3   *Cookson v Knowles* (1979) A.C. 556 (H.L.).

4   D. Kemp, 'The assessment of damages for future pecuniary loss in personal injury claims', *Civil Justice Quarterly*, 1984, pp. 120–32.

5   [1971] 2 All E.R. 1205, CA.

6   A. M. Parkman, 'The multiplier in English fatal accident cases: what happens when judges teach economics?', *International Review of Law and Economics*, 1985, 5: 187–97.

(£1,255), and assuming that he worked until retirement at 65, that productivity grew at 1 per cent per year and using a discount rate of 2 per cent, the estimated loss to the injured victim at the date of injury would have been £36,438. If interest were added the figure would have increased to £48,262 at the time of trial in 1969, and to £54,243 at the time of the Court of Appeal decision in 1971. The final sum calculated using these reasonable assumptions is more than two and a half times that awarded to the plaintiff by the court.

Here is an instance where simple economics can not only improve the consistency of the law but also the welfare of accident victims. The fact that judges blatantly refused to employ standard financial techniques, such as compound interest and sensible discount rates, seems inexcusable. Indeed, this has now been recognised as inappropriate, and recent reforms have resulted in personal injury damages in the UK being placed on sounder actuarial principles using the so-called 'Ogden Tables'.

Nonetheless, in the estimation of future losses there is still a way to go to achieve full compensation through the English courts. Recent research based on compensation for personal injury in 100 court cases found that if better account had been taken of labour market information as used by US courts, there would have been an increase of 25 per cent on average in the compensation payments, although in one quarter of cases the award would have been lower.[7] The research found that compared with the US method of calculating future personal injury losses, the UK courts:

---

7   R. McNabb, R. Lewis, H. Robinson and V. Wass, 'Court awards for damages for loss of future earnings: an empirical study and an alternative method of calculation', *Journal of Law and Society*, 2002, 29: 409–35; R. McNabb, R. Lewis and V. Wass, 'Methods for calculating damages for loss of future earnings', *Journal of Personal Injury Law*, 2002, pp. 151–65.

- consistently under-compensate men;
- underestimate the impact of disability on post-injury earnings potential, and therefore under-compensate on this account;
- may under-compensate people from ethnic minorities for future loss of earnings; and
- do not always determine the 'multiplier' accurately.

English courts do not use economists or economic techniques to assist in calculating future losses. This contrasts graphically with the US courts, which for some time have used economists and sometimes sophisticated statistical techniques, such as hedonic regressions, to estimate the losses of those injured. This has given rise to expert testimony by economists[8] in personal injury litigation, and the subject of 'forensic economics'.[9]

The economics of crime

Crime is undeniably an economic problem, and a serious one. In 2003/04 there were 16.4 million recorded offences against individuals and households in England and Wales, imposing annual direct losses and costs of the criminal justice system estimated at £60 billion.[10] Put simply, the material welfare of society would be considerably greater if crime did not exist, or was reduced. The economic approach to crime and the criminal law casts the economist in the roles of both technician *and* supertechnician. As a technician the economist has produced a mass of empirical evidence

---

8   D. B. Dobbs, *Handbook on the Law of Remedies*, West Publishing, St Paul, 1973.

9   See generally the *Journal of Forensic Economics*.

10 S. Brand and R. Price, *The Economic and Social Costs of Crime*, Home Office Research Paper 217, 2005.

to support the proposition that criminal penalties deter crime. As a supertechnician the economist has suggested ways in which the criminal law and its procedures can be improved to increase their cost-effectiveness in crime prevention and the administration of the system of criminal justice.

Theory and empirics of deterrence

The economic approach to crime is based, as one would expect, on the assumption that criminals, victims and law enforcers are rational. The decision to engage in crime is seen as no different in character from that of choosing a job. An individual participates in criminal activity because it offers a stream of net benefits greater than that of legitimate uses of his time and effort. 'Persons become "criminals"', states Gary Becker, 'not because their basic motivations differ from that of other persons, but because their benefits and costs differ.'[11]

The economists' model of crime 'predicts' *inter alia* that as the sanctions meted out by the law increase the attractiveness of participation in illicit activities decreases, and less will take place. That is, criminal sanctions deter crime.

Economists have not stopped at this controversial claim. Beginning with the work of Isaac Ehrlich[12] in the USA, there has been a raft of statistical studies that broadly confirm the economists' deterrence model. Moreover, these studies have often provided estimates of the impact on crime of changes in enforcement activity and penalties.

---

11 G. S. Becker, 'Crime and punishment: an economic approach', *Journal of Political Economy*, 1968, 76: 167–217.

12 I. Ehrlich, 'Participation in illegitimate activities: a theoretical and empirical investigation', *Journal of Political Economy*, 1973, 81: 521–64.

David Pyle, for example, has undertaken one such statistical study of property crime in England and Wales. Within an explicitly formulated economic model of crime he has examined the impact on the incidence of property crime of changes in key enforcement variables (the number of police, conviction rate and length of imprisonment), the economic gains from illegal activity, and the unemployment rate. The results support the predictions of the economic model; those variables which increased the expected penalty tended to reduce the incidence of property crimes while those which increased the gains to illegal activity or decreased the gains to legitimate activity have the opposite effect. Further, through the use of empirical analysis Pyle has been able to measure the impact on the incidence of crime of a 10 per cent increase in enforcement and other variables. Figure 1 summarises the impact of a 10 per cent increase in each enforcement variable on the rate of different property crimes.

This type of research has extended to the 'death penalty', where it has also identified a statistically significant deterrent effect. The first such statistical study was by Isaac Ehrlich,[13] who estimated that one extra execution annually deters eight murders. This attracted considerable notoriety and deep controversy because Ehrlich's research was cited in the US Supreme Court in *Gregg v Georgia*,[14] which reintroduced the death penalty in the USA. Wolpin's study of crime rates in England and Wales from 1928 to 1968 found similarly when it showed that when the death

---

13   I. Ehrlich, 'The deterrent effect of capital punishment: a question of life and death', *American Economic Review*, 1975, 65: 397–417.

14   428 US 153 Supreme Court (1976).

Figure 1 **The effect on the rate of property crimes of a 10 per cent increase in five variables: numbers of police officers, rate of imprisonment, length of imprisonment, illegal gains and unemployment rate**

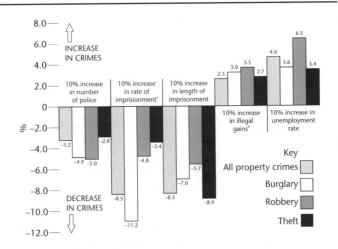

Notes: a) the rate of imprisonment refers to the proportion of convicted offenders who are sentenced to immediate imprisonment; b) an increase in illegal gains, or profits from crime, is measured by the rateable value per head

Source: D. J. Pyle, 'The economics of crime in Britain', *Economic Affairs*, December 1988/January 1989, 9(2): 8–9

penalty existed, one execution prevented four murders![15] More recent research using better data and controls for other factors[16] – such as distinguishing premeditated murder and crimes of

15   K. I. Wolpin, 'An economic analysis of crime and punishment in England and Wales, 1894–1967', *Journal of Political Economy*, 1978, 86: 815–40.

16   H. Dezhbakhsh, P. H. Rubin and J. M. Shephard, 'Does capital punishment have a deterrent effect? New evidence from postmoratorium panel data', *American Law and Economics Review*, 2003, 5: 344–76.

passion – finds that in the USA one execution deterred an estimated eighteen murders, with a 10 per cent margin of error, i.e. between a minimum of ten and a maximum of 28 avoided homicides. It should be noted that this does not mean that the death penalty is the most effective or cost-effective deterrent, or the principal explanation of the murder rate. Often the statistical analysis shows that other factors (such as labour market conditions) are equally or more important, and that imposing the death penalty is expensive.

Optimal deterrence

If criminals are deterred by the penalties meted out by the law, then society must decide the type and size of the penalties for various crimes. For the economist these matters will be determined by the extent to which different types of penalties (fines, imprisonment, community service, and so on) deter crime, compared with the respective costs of each sanction.

Results like those calculated by Pyle are a valuable input into evaluating the cost-effectiveness of different policies to reduce crime.[17] In Table 1 the results of Pyle's statistical study are matched to the costs of each enforcement activity in achieving a 1 per cent reduction in the incidence of property crime. They show that reducing crime by employing more police is not cost-effective. To achieve a 1 per cent reduction in property crime by greater policing would require an annual expenditure of over £51 million. This is ten times the cost of achieving the same reduction through an increase in the imprisonment rate or the length of imprisonment.

---

17 D. J. Pyle, *An Economic Model of Recorded Property Crimes in England and Wales*, PhD thesis, University of Leicester, 1984; Pyle, 'The economics of crime in Britain', *Economic Affairs*, January 1989, 9: 6–9.

Table 1 **Estimated costs of reducing property crimes by 1
per cent**

	Policy option	Cost (£ million)
Either	Increase number of police officers[a]	51.2
or	Increase number of people sentenced to imprisonment[b]	4.9
or	Increase average length of imprisonment[b]	3.6

Notes: a) the cost of employing an additional police officer is estimated at £16,000 per annum; b) the cost of keeping someone in prison is estimated to be £15,000 per annum

Source: D. J. Pyle, 'The economics of crime in Britain', *Economic Affairs*, December 1988/January 1989, 9(2): 6–9

A simple model assists in providing some potential policy prescriptions. The penalty that influences a criminal's actions and decision to participate in a crime is the product of two elements, the severity of the sanction and the frequency with which it is imposed on offenders. By multiplying these factors we obtain the expected penalty. Thus, if the penalty is a fine of £200 but only 50 per cent of offenders are apprehended and convicted, then the expected penalty is £100 ($0.5 \times £200 = £100$). If criminals are risk neutral, that is they evaluate risky prospects solely in terms of the expected value of an increase or decrease in their wealth, the same level of deterrence can be achieved by reducing either the level of the fine or its likelihood, provided there is a compensating increase in the other. Thus, a 50 per cent chance of a £200 fine ($0.5 \times £200 = £100$) brings about the same level of deterrence as a 25 per cent prospect of a £400 fine ($0.25 \times £400 = £100$). In each case the expected fine is £100. Thus, there are different combinations of conviction rate and severity of sanctions which will achieve the same level of deterrence.

The optimal combination of the conviction rate and the severity of the penalty is, in the economic model, determined by their respective costs. Apprehending and convicting offenders is very costly – it requires manpower, considerable time and equipment. Sanctions, on the other hand, deter by the *threat* that they will be imposed. Thus, the costs of enforcing the criminal law and deterring crime can be lowered by progressively increasing the severity of the fine while reducing the conviction rate.

These types of cost considerations suggest the form punishment should take. Simplistically there should be a reliance on cheaper types of sanctions. This leads to a preference for monetary fines rather than imprisonment or other custodial sanctions. Fines are easy to calculate and involve a simple transfer payment from the offender to the state which can be used to compensate the victim and defray the costs of the police and the courts. Imprisonment adds avoidable costs, such as the investment in prisons, the wages of warders and probationary officers, and the value of the offender's lost production in legitimate activities. Society gains nothing from this form of punishment when the alternative of costless monetary fines is available.

What has been outlined is the so-called 'case for fines'. Namely, the costs of achieving a given level of deterrence can be reduced by lowering the level of enforcement activity and raising the severity of the punishment. Further, the punishment should take the form, where possible, of high monetary fines because they deter crime costlessly.[18] This leads to the policy prescription of very high penalties many multiples of the harm inflicted and

---

18   A. M. Polinsky and S. Shavell, 'The economic theory of public enforcement of the law', *Journal of Economic Literature*, 2000, 38: 45–76.

a relatively low detection/conviction rate. That is, a public enforcement agency that has optimal deterrence as a primary goal will be guided to conserve enforcement costs by adopting a penal enforcement strategy – a 'boil them in oil' approach – which rarely prosecutes offenders but when it does imposes a draconian penalty. For example, if the conviction rate is 1 per cent then a fine 100 times the damages inflicted would be required to achieve optimal deterrence.

Clearly, with the exception of some administrative sanctions (such as treble damages under US antitrust law), this deterrence multiplier approach is not used, and historically the penalties imposed on criminals have declined in severity as public enforcement and its effectiveness have increased. The reality is that fines and draconian penalties are not costless and distort incentives. Subsequent work by economists has refined the model to take account of other factors which point to a more moderate and discriminating system of incentives. Among the factors these models consider are:

- **Marginal deterrence.** If fines (or any sanctions) are draconian across the board, prospective lawbreakers will not be deterred from committing the more serious offences.[19] If stealing a loaf of bread or armed robbery both attract similar penalties, the law does little to discourage armed robbery. Differential fines must, therefore, be built into the criminal penalty system to create marginal deterrence of crimes imposing greater losses and harm.

---

19   G. J. Stigler, 'The optimum enforcement of laws', *Journal of Political Economy*, 1970, 78: 526–36.

- **Insolvency of wrongdoers.** Where prospective lawbreakers would be rendered insolvent, then high fines may not deter lawbreaking, and may in fact encourage more lawbreaking than a lower fine would because the lawbreaker appreciates that he will not have to pay if caught. This may justify custodial sentences.

- **Enforcement errors.** Errors in conviction are frequently made so that draconian penalties will over-deter. High fines may result in ruining the innocent, or deterring the wrong activities.

- **Costly fines.** Fines may not be costless, and very high fines can be expensive to enforce. They may channel the infringers' activities into more robust legal challenges of the enforcer's findings and quantification of fines. There may be disputes over their magnitude and a generalised feeling that the fines are disproportionate to the gravity of the offences, and this may encourage a generally litigious stance with the possible neutralisation of the law. This appears to be the case for EU administrative fines in antitrust, where the EU Commission's fining policy has led to legal appeals, costly litigation and invariably the reduction of fines by the courts.[20]

- **Nullification.** Severe penalties may also be nullified by judges and juries. One argument against the death penalty is that juries are more likely to find the guilty innocent than run the risk of inflicting a death sentence on an innocent person.

---

20 C. G. Veljanovski, 'Penalties for price-fixers – an analysis of fines imposed on 39 cartels under EC antitrust', *European Competition Law Review*, 2006, 26: 510–512.

These considerations lead to an extended cost–benefit assessment of fines and other penalties, which waters down the 'boil them in oil' prescription of the simpler model. Nonetheless, the basic proposition remains – the choice of enforcement activity and penalties is to be determined by their incentive effects and relative costs.

Defining legal terms

The most novel role the economist can adopt is that of *economic rhetorician*, or simply the economics of law. This applies economics to define legal terms, interpret laws and evaluate the effects of laws that do not have an obvious economic content or objective. It is 'concerned with the principle of economic efficiency as an explanatory tool by which existing legal rules and decisions may be rationalized or comprehended'.[21] Clearly, such economic theory will not be admissible in court, but it will be of use in developing a theory of law and of critically assessing the law. The lawyer is offered an entirely different vocabulary and categories that can be used to redefine legal terms. Concepts such as choice, trade-offs, incentive effects, marginal analysis, externalities, the cheapest cost avoider and others form the basis for each discussion. Areas of law are treated by functional categories such as distinctions between care and activity levels, alternative and joint care, accidents between strangers and those occurring in situations where the parties have a pre-existing 'exchange' relationship. Thus, instead of relying on judicial analysis and reasoning, an external conceptual framework

---

21   J. L. Coleman, 'Efficiency, exchange and auction: philosophical aspects of the economic approach to law', *California Law Review*, 1980, 68: 221.

is provided which cuts through the linguistic formulations of judges to offer different reasons or criticisms of the law.

It may seem an odd, not to say arrogant, contention to suggest that an economist is required to (re)interpret the words of judges before they can be understood. But the reason why this is a plausible endeavour is that common-law judges, especially those in England and Wales, rarely state general principles of law. The common law, which is the customary law of the land, evolved through decisions of judges in cases over centuries, is not based on a set of rules or a code. It is based on decisions in specific cases which are used as precedents for deciding subsequent cases. The common law has been described as a system of law that places a particular value on dissension, obscurity and the tentative character of judicial utterances so 'that uniquely authentic statements of the rule ... cannot be made'.[22] Thus, one of the principal activities of lawyers is to shift and categorise cases in order to distil the 'rules' of law. It is this 'murkiness' of the common law which has permitted economics to be used to suggest new definitions for key legal concepts.[23]

Tort

The economic analysis of tort provides the starting point for this use of economics. The law of torts governs whether or not victims of harms, such as road accidents, medical negligence, defamation and other third-party harms, should be compensated by those

22 B. Simpson, 'The common law and legal theory', in W. Twining (ed.), *Legal Theory and Common Law*, Blackwell, Oxford, 1986, p. 17.

23 For a discussion of this use of economics, see C. G. Veljanovski, 'Legal theory, economic analysis and the law of torts', in Twining, *Legal Theory*, op. cit., ch. 12; C. Veljanovski, *Economic Principles of Law*, Cambridge University Press, Cambridge, 2007 (in press).

who injure them. Economists view these occurrences as externalities or third-party effects generally occurring outside of direct contractual relationships, and where in the absence of the law these external or uncompensated costs are inflicted generating inefficiently high levels of harm and wrongdoing, i.e. social costs.

Under the common law, in most accident situations the injurer is held liable only if he or she has failed to exercise sufficient care – that is, has acted negligently or has been at 'fault'. The most famous statement of negligence in English (and Scottish) law is Lord Atkin's dictum in the 'snail-in-a-bottle' case of *Donoghue v Stevenson*:

> You must not injure your neighbour, and the lawyers' question: who is my neighbour? receives a restricted reply. You must take reasonable care to avoid acts or omissions which you can reasonably foresee would injure your neighbour. Who then, in law, is my neighbour? The answer seems to be persons who are so closely and directly affected by my act that I ought reasonably to have them in contemplation as being so affected when I am directing my mind to the acts and omissions.[24]

As stated, this judicial test is extremely vague. Its constituent parts are supplied by the decision of judges in specific cases over time. Yet the linguistic formulations used by judges such as 'duty of care', 'reasonable foreseeability', 'proximity' and 'reasonable care' have a chameleon-like quality. They are frequently used interchangeably, confusing lawyer and layman alike. The result is that the general principles of English common law are open-ended. The cases applying the law supply a patchwork of decisions where the underlying logic, if any, is not self-evident.

---

24 *Donoghue v Stevenson* (1932) A.C. 562, p. 58.

The Hand Test

Consider the way the courts determine the legal standard of care in negligence. The typical situation is that A (the defendant) has harmed B (the claimant) by some action resulting from lack of care on A's (and frequently B's) part. A drives carelessly, changing lanes and crashing into another vehicle, or a doctor leaves a pair of forceps in B's body during an operation.

An economist would assign the loss resulting from an accident to the party or parties most able to avoid it. The decision as to who should bear the loss would be made on the basis of the costs of avoidance to the claimant and defendant compared with the expected damages. Indeed, a US court decision by Judge Learned Hand explicitly formulates the standard of care in these terms. According to the 'Hand Test', the defendant's culpability is determined by balancing 'the burden of adequate precautions' (B) against 'the likelihood of an accident' (P) multiplied by the gravity of the harm should the accident occur (L).[25] If the cost of avoiding the accident (B) exceeds the expected harm ($P \times L$), then avoidance would increase costs. The Hand Test imposes liability on the defendant only if it can be established that accident avoidance is the cheapest solution (see Box 3). It mirrors closely the earlier discussion of the economics of safety.

The Hand Test is no aberration. It encapsulates the main considerations used by the courts in England and other Commonwealth countries, and most casebooks and texts use the three factors (risk, precautions and gravity) to organise their discussion of the cases.[26] The Hand Test can be regarded

---

25 *United States v Carroll Towing Co.* 159 F. 2d. 169, 173 (2d Cir.), 1947.

26 Hand-like statements of the breach of duty test can be found in *Mackintosh* v. *Mackintosh* (1864), 2 M. 1357; *Ryan v Fisher* (1976) 51 ALJR 125; *Morris v West Hartlepool Steam Navigation Co.* (1956) HL 574/5.

as a convenient summary of the factors relevant to determining whether the defendant has breached his duty to take reasonable care for the protection of others. To illustrate this point, consider some of the classic cases familiar to all English law students.

Under the Hand Test the defendant is more likely to be found in breach of his duty if the costs of care are low, the risks of injury high and the severity of the injuries, should an accident occur, also high. It is the interplay of these three factors which is important to the decision whether the defendant has breached his duty of care. As we shall see, all these factors are important in law.

The likelihood of injury (L) is a relevant factor in determining whether the risk created by the defendant is unreasonable. In *Fardon v Harcourt-Rivington*,[27] Lord Dunedin stated that 'people must guard against reasonable probabilities, but they are not bound to guard against fantastic possibilities'.

In *Bolton v Stone*[28] a batsman hit a ball over a fence on to an adjoining highway, injuring the plaintiff. In the 90-year period over which cricket had been played on the field no one had ever been injured, and in the previous 30 years the ball had been hit over the fence only six times. The House of Lords found the defendant not liable because the chance of injury 'was very small'. Lord Reid applied the following test: 'whether the risk of damage to a person on the road was so small that a reasonable man …, considering the matter from the view of safety, would have thought it right to refrain from taking steps to prevent the danger'.

---

27   [1932] 146 L.T. 391.
28   [1951] 1 All ER 1078.

Box 3 **Economic application of the Hand Test**

'In *United States v Carroll Towing Co.* 159 F.2d 169 (2d Cir. 1947), the question was presented whether it was negligent for the Conners Company, the owner of a barge, to leave it unattended for several hours in a busy harbour. While unattended, the barge broke away from its moorings and collided with another ship. Judge Learned Hand stated for the court (at page 173):

There is no general rule to determine when the absence of a bargee or other attendant will make the owner of the barge liable for injuries to other vessels if she breaks away from her moorings ... It becomes apparent why there can be no such general rule, when we consider the grounds for such a liability. Since there are occasions when every vessel will break from her moorings, and since, if she does, she becomes a menace to those about her, the owner's duty, as in other similar situations, to provide against resulting injuries is a function of three variables: (1) The probability that she will break away; (2) the gravity of the resulting injury, if she does; (3) the burden of adequate precautions. Possibly it serves to bring this notion into relief to state it in algebraic terms: if the probability be called P; the injury L; and the burden B; liability depends upon whether B is less than L multiplied by P: i.e., whether $B < PL$ ... In the case at bar the bargee left at five o'clock on the afternoon of January 3rd, and the flotilla broke away at about two o'clock in the afternoon of the following day, twenty-one hours afterwards. The bargee had been away all the time, and we hold that his fabricated story was affirmative evidence that he had no excuse for his absence. At the locus in quo – especially during the short January days and in the full tide of war activity – barges were being constantly 'drilled' in and out. Certainly it was not beyond reasonable expectation that, with the inevitable haste and bustle, the work might not be done with adequate care. In

such circumstances we hold – and it is all that we do hold
– that it was a fair requirement that the Conners Company
should have a bargee aboard (unless he had some excuse
for his absence), during the working hours of daylight.

'By redefinition of two terms in the Hand formula it is
easy to bring out its economic character. B, the burden of
precautions, is the cost of avoiding the accident, while L, the
loss if the accident occurs, is the cost of the accident itself. P
times L (P × L) – the cost of the accident if it occurs, multiplied
(or, as is sometimes said, "discounted") by the probability that
the accident will occur – is what an economist would call the
"expected cost" of the accident. Expected cost is most easily
understood as the average cost that will be incurred over
a period of time long enough for the predicted number of
accidents to be the actual number.

'For example, if the probability that a certain type of
accident will occur is .001 (one in a thousand) and the accident
cost if it does occur is $10,000, the expected accident cost is
$10 ($10,000 × .001); and this is equivalent to saying that if
we observe the activity that gives rise to this type of accident
for a long enough period of time we will observe an average
accident cost of $10. Suppose the activity in question is
automobile trips from point A to point B. If there are 100,000
trips, there will be 100 accidents, assuming that our probability
of .001 was correct. The total cost of the 100 accidents will be
$1 million ($10,000 × 100). The average cost, which is simply
the total cost ($1 million) divided by the total number of trips
(100,000), will be $10. This is the same as the expected cost.'[29]

29 R. A. Posner, *Tort Law – Cases and Economic Analysis*, Little, Brown, Boston, MA,
1982, p. 1.

In economic terms the risk of injury was very small so that the damage was discounted very heavily (i.e. P x L is very low). Also, the facts in the case show that the fence was already 29 feet high (it was a 12-foot fence built on a 17-foot rise), so that the costs of avoiding such an accident were bound to be very high (hence B is considerably greater than $P \times L$).

In *Haley v London Electricity Board*[30] the factors in the Hand equation are discussed more fully. The defendant (the LEB) was excavating a pavement and as a precaution placed a punner (a wooden tool for ramming earth) around a post to make it firm at one end of the excavation on the completion of the day's work. The claimant, who was blind and could avoid ordinary obstacles only with the aid of a white stick, missed the punner and tripped. As a result he hit his head and became deaf. In this case the defendant alleged that the chance of a blind man coming along the road that day was small and that therefore it was not reasonable to expect him to take precautions. Lord Reid did not agree. Evidence was presented that one in 500 people in London at the time were blind. He went on to consider the costs of taking adequate precautions. Padded lamp-posts, for example, were not justified in view of the risks. But he continued: 'A moment's reflection ... shows that a low obstacle in an unusual place is a grave danger: on the other hand, it is clear that quite a light fence some two feet high is adequate warning. There would be no difficulty in providing such a fence here.'[31]

The standard of care required of the defendant will tend to rise with the magnitude of the harm. In *Paris v Stepney Borough*

---

30 [1964] 3 All ER 185.
31 The reason why such a fence was not provided by the LEB was that it arrived late.

Council[32] a one-eyed man was blinded when a chip of metal lodged in his good eye. The claimant argued that his employer was negligent in failing to supply him with goggles even though these were not usually provided to employees. The court held that, although it would not have been negligent not to provide full-sighted employees with goggles, it was in this case because the consequences were more serious. In Lord Morton's judgment he stated that 'the more serious the damage which will happen if an accident occurs, the more thorough are the precautions which employers must take'. He also made it clear that the right-hand side of the Hand Test (P × L) is relevant: 'In considering generally the precautions that the employer ought to take for the protection of his workmen it must, in my view, be right to take into account both elements, the likelihood of an accident happening and the gravity of the consequences.'

The cost of reducing risk is explicitly referred to in other cases. In *Watt v Hertfordshire County Council*[33] Lord Denning stated that in measuring due care one must balance the risk against the measures necessary to eliminate it. If the costs of precautions are minimal, liability is more likely to follow. In the Australian case, *Mercer v Commissioner for Road Transport and Tramways*,[34] the driver of a tram collapsed at the controls and, despite the efforts of the conductor to stop it with the handbrakes, a collision resulted. The claimant alleged that a 'dead man's handle' which automatically stops a train if released would have avoided the accident. The court held that, in terms of the risk that would be avoided, the costs would be disproportionate.

---

32 [1951] 1 All ER 42.

33 [1954] 2 All ER 368, 371.

34 [1937] 56 CLR 580.

Sometimes the courts will excuse the defendant's conduct if it has a high 'social utility'. In *Daborn v Bath Tramways Motor Co. Ltd and T. Smithey*[35] the claimant was driving a left-hand-drive ambulance. The claimant gave a signal but collided with a bus. Here several issues were discussed. Counsel for the defendants argued that 'the driver of such a car should, before executing a turn, stop his car, move to the right-hand seat and look backwards to see if another car was attempting to overtake him and then start up again'. Lord Asquith was satisfied both that this procedure would involve possible delay and that it might be ineffective. The court considered another cost. It was a time of national emergency requiring all transport resources to be employed. The risk could have been eliminated by forbidding such vehicles to be used. But, as the judge pointed out, this cost must be weighed against the reduction in risk.

Daborn is an application of the opportunity cost concept. In *Daborn* the cost of prohibiting left-hand-drive ambulances was the forgone social benefits. And the opportunity cost of forbearing from using these ambulances (B in terms of the Hand formulation) had to be compared with the reduction in (total) expected losses from using them.

Economic model of negligence

The Hand Test is not an entirely accurate representation of the economics of negligence or the way the courts decide negligence. Care is not an on/off situation – it is a *continuum* of more or less care or actions that reduce the likelihood of an accident. The Hand Test is misleading on this account. As stated it gave the

---

35   [1946] 2 All ER 333, CA.

impression that greater care would avoid the victim's loss completely. While this may be true in some cases, it is generally not. From an economic viewpoint optimal care or deterrence is defined as a situation where an additional £1 spent on safety decreases expected loss by £1 – that is, actual loss discounted by the *reduction* in the likelihood of the accident occurring (point C* in Figure 2). That is to say, we make comparisons with marginal or incremental costs, not total costs and expected losses.

Consider the following example. Suppose that my house is on a particularly sharp bend on the road so that visitors must negotiate an acute angle to turn into my drive. A number of visitors have damaged their cars entering my drive. Assume that the risk of damage is one in ten and that damage to vehicles averages about £100. If I move one of the fence posts I can reduce the likelihood that future visitors will damage their cars from one in ten to one in twenty. Assume that it costs me only £2 to move the post. Should I move it and, if I do not, should I be found negligent? The answer is 'yes'. It costs me £2 to move the post but, as a result, I save my visitors 5 per cent of £100 = £5. Thus, in determining whether the plaintiff has been negligent, we must compare the costs of the actions that could have been taken against the reduction in the risks that these bring about. That is, the comparison is between the *marginal* costs of greater care and the *marginal* reduction in expected losses. If marginal safety costs are less than marginal expected loss, more care is economically efficient, and the defendant should be held liable (in Figure 2 care less than C*). If the next unit of care costs £2 but avoids only £1 of damage, excessive precautions have been taken and no damages should be awarded.

In practice, courts do decide negligence cases in this way, albeit less formally and rigorously. Even though the judge makes

Figure 2　**The way an economist sees negligence**

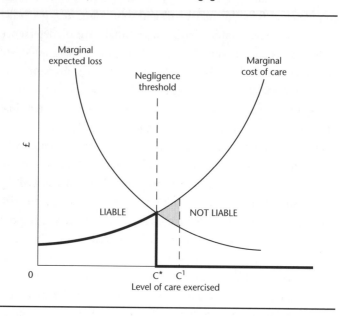

a binary choice (guilty/not guilty), the grounds upon which he decides fault are incremental. The judge determines whether or not the defendant has acted unreasonably. But this disguises the way the courts determine fault and how lawyers present their clients' cases. The adversarial style of common-law adjudication forces the lawyer and judge to think not in terms of absolutes but in terms of incremental actions. To establish fault the claimant has to persuade the judge that on the balance of probabilities the defendant did not act with reasonable care. The claimant will enumerate actions which, had the defendant taken them, would have avoided the accident. The defendant will counter with reasons why this would not have reduced the likelihood of harm or would have been impractical, too expensive and unreasonable. The *basis* on which the judge decides and the process by which he arrives at this decision are very similar to the way in which an economist would *approach* the problem. The courts, in effect, engage in a 'cost–benefit' analysis.

A good judicial application of marginal cost analysis can be found in *Latimer v AEC Ltd.*[36] The respondent's factory was flooded by an unusually heavy thunderstorm and a collection of water and oil collected on the floor. Sawdust was spread on the floor but there was too little to deal with the (large) quantity of water. The court held that there was enough sawdust to meet any situation that could have been foreseen. The appellant, who was working on the night shift, was injured when he slipped on a wet, oily patch, crushing his leg, while trying to load a barrel on to a trolley. This case illustrates nicely the fact that the courts take into account the costs of additional care and balance them against the incremental reduction in risks. The issue before the court was whether a 'reasonably prudent employer would have closed down the factory rather than allow his employees to run the risks involved in continuing work'. Lord Tucker decided the danger was not such as to require the factory to close. In economic terms Lord Tucker was comparing the additional costs of closedown against the incremental reduction of the risks of injury to workers. In terms of Figure 2 the court felt that the employer was at C^* (the economically efficient level of care). To require the shutdown of the factory (care level C^2) would have imposed a cost burden on the employer not fully offset by the gain to workers (the excess cost is the shaded area).

---

36   [1983] 2 All ER 449.

6 COMPETITION LAW

Competition or antitrust law has a pervasive effect on business. A day rarely passes without the launch of another investigation of a firm, industry or practice by a national competition authority or the European Commission.[1] Recent examples include excessive credit card, bank and mobile phone charges, Microsoft's alleged blocking of its competitors from using its Windows operating system, large fines imposed on pharmaceutical companies for price fixing, and a constant stream of merger investigations. All these raise concerns that the companies involved have acted, or may in the future act, in a way that restricts competition and ultimately raises prices to consumers. Competition and merger laws seek to prevent this.[2] Translating the pro-competition goals into effective law has often not been easy because regulators work with different theories of competition and competitive harm, and there are often sharply different views about the facts in specific cases.

What is not in dispute has been the phenomenal rise of competition laws. At the time the first edition of this book was written

---

1   European competition and merger laws are enforced by the European Commission's competition directorate general, known as DG COMP.

2   R. W. Crandall and C. Winston, 'Does antitrust improve consumer welfare? Assessing the evidence', *Journal of Economic Perspectives*, 2003, 17: 3–26; S. Davies and A. Majumdar, *The Development of Targets for Consumer Savings Arising from Competition Policy*, Economics Discussion Paper 4, OFT 386, 2002.

very few countries had competition laws; now very few do not: at the last count over 100 countries.

Many of these countries have adopted EC competition law, which is the law of the 25 countries of the European Union. EC law is remarkably brief. It consists of three Articles of the EC Treaty – Article 81 (anti-competitive agreements and cartels), Article 82 (abuse of dominance or monopolisation) and Article 87 (state aids) – and the EC Merger Regulation. In addition, each country in the EU has its own national competition and merger laws based on the EU competition laws, but often with local variations and different enforcement practices.

The rise of the economic approach

Economics is now central to EU and US competition and merger laws.[3] Richard Whish, a respected legal academic, displays English understatement when he comments: 'Competition law is about economics and economic behaviour, and it is essential for anyone involved in the subject – whether as a lawyer, regulator, civil servant or in any capacity – to have some knowledge of the economic concepts concerned.'[4]

Chief Judge Posner, writing in 2001, is more exuberant when he declared that 'Today, [US] antitrust law is a body of economically rational principles',[5] continuing:

---

3   P. Nicoliades, 'An essay on economics and the competition law of the European Community', *Legal Issues of European Integration*, 2000, 27: 7–27; W. E. Kovacic and C. Shapiro, 'Antitrust policy: a century of economic and legal thinking', *Journal of Economic Perspectives*, 2000, 14: 43–60.

4   R. Whish, *Competition Law*, 5th edn, Lexis Nexis, London, 2003, p. 1.

5   R. A. Posner, *Antitrust*, 2nd edn, University of Chicago Press, Chicago, 2001, p. viii.

> Almost everyone professionally involved in antitrust today
> – whether as litigator, prosecutor, judge, academic, or
> informed observer – not only agrees that the only goal of
> antitrust laws should be to promote economic welfare, but
> agrees on the central tenets of economic theory that should
> be used to determine the consistency of specific business
> practices with that goal.[6]

While economics may not have supplanted law, law and economics are now so intertwined in European antitrust and merger laws that it is not possible to talk about legal and economic approaches; just good and bad economic approaches. Further, the rise of the economic approach has seen economists playing more active roles as regulators, policy advisers and experts assisting lawyers and regulators to apply the law, and to defend companies and others against prosecution, and more recently damage claims (Box 4).

There has always been an 'economic' basis for antitrust influenced by past economic theories mixed with pluralistic, social and industrial goals. The result was competition laws that pursued a number of different, often contradictory, objectives and lacked economic logic. The break came in the 1950s when price theory was applied to the problems of US antitrust. One such influential approach was the Structure Conduct Performance (SCP) approach, or 'Harvard School', associated with Edward Mason and Joe Bain,[7] and in the legal field with Carl Kaysen and Donald Turner.[8] As the name implies, it viewed firm and market performance

---

6   Ibid., p. ix.

7   J. E. Bain, *Industrial Organization*, Wiley, New York, 1959.

8   C. Kaysen and D. F. Turner, *Antitrust Policy*, Harvard University Press, Cambridge, MA, 1959.

Box 4 Adam Smith in court

Alfred Taubman, the ex-chairman of Sotheby's, the art auction house, unsuccessfully appealed his conviction for price fixing. The prosecutors had said that Adam Smith knew what was going on, even if his death in 1790 prevented him from appearing at the trial as an expert witness. They quoted Smith's words from the *Wealth of Nations*: 'People of the same trade seldom meet together, even for merriment and diversion, but the conversation ends in a conspiracy against the public, or in some contrivance to raise prices.' Taubman's lawyers argued that 'the risk that the jury might make the impermissible leap from the mere fact of the meetings to Taubman's guilt was exponentially increased when the government decided to use quasi-expert testimony from renowned economist Adam Smith'. The court rejected this argument, stating 'the government did not offer the quotation as a statement of law. Instead, the prosecutor specifically explained to the jury that Smith was "not a witness here" and that his statement was nothing more than "insight" that was proven correct in this case . . .'. Taubman's defence lawyers could well have reflected (but without offering any assistance to their client) on the rest of Adam Smith's quote: 'It is impossible indeed to prevent such meetings, by any law which either be executed, or would be consistent with liberty and justice.'[9]

9   *US v A. Alfred Taubman* 297 F.3d 161, 59 Fed. R. Evid. Serv. 211, 2002-2 Trade Cases P 73, 753.

as predetermined by industry structure. Considerable research failed, however, to find strong correlations between industry structure and high profitability and other indicators of monopoly. Also, the law at the time reflected a rigidity and inclination to treat a number of industry practices that involved restrictions or exclusions as per se anti-competitive. Thus vertical restraints between, say, a producer and its distributors were treated as per se antitrust offences, irrespective of whether or not the consumers benefited or the producer earned 'excess' profits. This also reflected the economists' then focus on monopoly and market failure. As Ronald Coase has commented:

> ... the preoccupation with the monopoly problem is that if an economist finds something – a business practice of one sort or another – that he does not understand, he looks for a monopoly explanation. And as in this field we are very ignorant, the number of un-understandable practices tends to be very large, and the reliance on monopoly explanation, frequent.[10]

Faced with little corroborative evidence, the SCP began to yield to the Chicago Approach. This questioned the then prevailing orthodoxy and subjected it to rigorous economic analysis and empirical research. It showed that many of the claims were flawed – many of the restrictions when rigorously analysed were often more likely to be efficient and contribute to greater consumers' welfare. Today the economic approach has at its core the application of rigorous price theory to investigate firm and market behaviour, and the operation of the law.

The rise of the 'economic approach' in Europe is more recent. Unlike in the USA it did not arise from an intellectual movement

---

10 R. Coase, 'Industrial organization: a proposal for research', in V. Fuchs (ed.), *Policy Issues and Research Opportunities in Industrial Organization*, National Bureau of Economic Research, New York, 1972.

or academic criticism.[11] Rather, it evolved slowly and drew largely from US developments and enforcement practices. A watershed came in 1997 when the European Commission published its Notice on market definition,[12] which borrowed heavily from the US *Horizontal Merger Guidelines*[13], and the activities of the European Commission's Merger Task Force, which championed the introduction of economics. While there was a greater acceptance of economics and economists, they were not central.

It was at the beginning of the millennium that the economic approach took hold as part of the European Commission's 'modernisation programme' of competition and merger laws. Two developments catapulted economics to the forefront. The first was a clash between US and EU antitrust authorities over the nature and purpose of competition law generated by the GE/Honeywell merger (see below), and the second the European Court of First Instance's (CFI) annulment in quick succession of not one but three European Commission merger decisions[14] in the space of several months in 2002. This was the first time the European Commission had ever lost an appeal in this area, and it sent shock waves through the directorate.

---

11 An early collaborative effort between economist and lawyer in the UK is R. B. Stevens and B. S. Yamey, *The Restrictive Trade Prices Court*, Weidenfeld & Nicolson, London, 1965.

12 EU *Commission Notice on the definition of the relevant market for the purposes of Community competition law*, 1997/C372/05.

13 US Department of Justice/Federal Trade Commission, *Horizontal Merger Guidelines* (1982, rev. 1997). Also Department of Justice, '20th anniversary of the 1982 Merger Guidelines: the contribution of the Merger Guidelines to the evolution of antitrust doctrine'.

14 Case T-342/99 *Airtours v Commission* (2002); Case T-310/01 *Schneider Electric v Commission* (2002); Case T-5/02 *Tetra Laval BV v Commission* (2002).

The CFI was uncompromising in its criticism of the European Commission's approach. It found that it had ridden roughshod over the facts, failed to satisfy the requisite standard of proof, and had not undertaken adequate factual and economic analyses. The response was that the proposed reforms of EU competition law went farther and deeper – a new EC Merger Regulation,[15] the reformulation of the legal standard for mergers from 'dominance' to 'significantly impeding effective competition',[16] the appointment of the first Chief Economist to the European Commission's competition directorate, the rewriting of guidelines which made clear that the purpose of competition law intervention is to be economic and to promote consumer welfare, and the decentralisation of competition law enforcement to the member states, and its privatisation by allowing those harmed to claim damages through the courts. To quote the European Competition Commissioner, Neelie Kroes:

> Consumer welfare is now well established as the standard the Commission applies when assessing mergers and infringements of the Treaty rules on cartels and monopolies. Our aim is simple: protect competition in the market as a means of enhancing consumer welfare and ensuring an efficient allocation of resources. An effects-based approach, grounded in solid economics, ensures that citizens enjoy the benefits of a competitive, dynamic market economy.[17]

15 Council Regulation (EC) No. 139/2004 on control of concentrations between undertakings. This replaced Regulation 4064/89 on 1 May 2004.

16 EU *Commission Guidelines on the assessment of horizontal mergers under the Council Regulation on the control of concentrations between undertakings*, 2000/C 31/03 (2004).

17 N. Kroes, 'European competition policy – delivering better markets and better choices', speech to European Consumer and Competition Day, 15 September 2005.

In European competition circles the 'economic approach' is now a key talking point.[18] This, as discussed, was not due to economists in the Commission or in academia, but of Europe's judges. The result has been a step-change in EC law from a form-based, structural approach (see below) to one that, to use the prevailing jargon, is effects- and fact-based, and aims to promote consumer rather than competitor welfare. That is, an approach that must now seek out the actual or likely competitive effects of various practices and mergers,[19] rather than the past over-reliance on presumption, form and theory (even economic theory) that size and concentration alone somehow imply anti-competitive abuse.

Why do we need competition law?

The basic justification for competition law is the existence of market power created and sustained by barriers to entry.[20] Market power can be defined as the ability of a firm or group of firms to

18 *An Economic Approach to Article 82 – Report by the Economic Advisory Group on Competition Policy (EAGCP)*, July 2005.

19 *Quantitative Techniques in Competition Analysis*, UK Office of Fair Trading Research Paper no. 17, 1999; J. B. Baker and D. L. Rubinfeld, 'Empirical methods in antitrust litigation: review and critique', *American Law and Economics Review*, 1999, 1: 386–435; International Competition Network, 'Role of economists and economic evidence in merger analysis', 2003, at www.internationalcompetitionnetwork.org/Role%20of%20Economists.pdf. For recent examples from US merger decisions see J. E. Kowka, Jr, and L. J. White (eds), *The Antitrust Revolution*, 4th edn, Oxford University Press, Oxford, 2004. Chief Justice Posner, referring to econometric analysis used in *FTC v Staples Inc.* 970 F. Supp. 1066 (D.D.C. 1997), declared that 'Economic analysis of mergers had come of age' (Posner, *Antitrust*, op. cit., p. 158).

20 M. Motta, *Competition Policy – Theory and Evidence*, Cambridge University Press, Cambridge, 2004.

profitably raise price above the competitive price by reducing output. Perhaps the best definition is contained in a dated 1955 report on US antitrust law:

> The basic characteristic of effective competition in the economic sense is that no one seller, and no group of sellers acting in concert, has the power to choose its level of profits by giving less and charging more. Where there is workable competition, rival sellers, whether existing competitors or new or potential entrants in the field, would keep this power in check by offering or threatening to offer effective inducements.[21]

The emphasis of 'giving less and charging more' is related to the slope of the market demand curve facing firms (see Figure 3 on page 116). It follows from the economists' postulate that the demand curves are negatively sloped (the higher the price, the lower the quantity demanded) so that the exercise of market power will be associated both with a price above the competitive level and a simultaneous reduction in the quantity of the product sold. That is, prices can only be raised if output is reduced! While this monopoly model indicates that excessive prices are the evil, all but a few dominance cases involve allegations of excessive prices. They tend to concern so-called exclusionary conduct – that is, blocking and harming competitors – sometimes by charging prices below the competitive price (called 'predatory pricing').

Market power can impose one or more of three types of avoidable economic losses: excessive production costs (x-inefficiency); excessive prices leading to the loss of consumers' surplus

---

21 *Report of the United States Attorney-General's National Committee to Study the Antitrust Laws*, 1955, p. 320.

(allocative inefficiency); and wasted resources in acquiring and/or maintaining market power (rent-seeking):

- **X-inefficiency** – The economist Sir John Hicks once quipped that the best monopoly profit was 'a quiet life'. Immune from competitive pressures, the monopolist may be less vigilant in containing costs so that over time it becomes bloated and inefficient. This leads to economic waste, misallocates resources and ultimately is paid for by the consumer in higher prices and lower output.
- **Excessive prices** – A monopolist restricts output to raise price above the competitive level. This action of, in effect, creating artificial scarcity imposes excessive prices, which has two effects – it redistributes wealth from consumers to the monopolist (a transfer effect which most economists are happy to ignore), and the higher price chokes off demand for a good that is cheaper to produce than the competitive price (the deadweight loss). It is the latter which represents the social costs of monopoly in a static world: consumers' willingness to pay above the marginal costs of production of the output not produced by the monopolist (Figure 3).
- **Rent-seeking** – Rent-seeking is unproductive profit-seeking induced by the prospect of acquiring or maintaining monopoly profits.[22] In the real world monopolies and cartels

---

22 The term comes from the notion of Ricardian rent on land. Since the supply of land, crudely defined, is fixed, the returns will not be affected by competitive forces but by the inherent scarcity. Thus land will yield a return above the normal return, known as an 'economic rent', which is not competed away. Such economic rents occur in other areas, most notably in the case of very talented sportsman (for example, David Beckham), actors, singers and other professionals who have talents that cannot be replicated.

do not just happen; they are created, either by favourable legislation or by concerted and costly efforts by firms over a period of time. The prospect of excessive profits from market power and immunity from competition gives firms a strong incentive to invest in gaining and protecting monopoly positions. It would be rational for firms or an industry group (cartel) to invest in lobbying and other market foreclosure actions just slightly below the anticipated wealth transfer from favourable legislation. Thus, the transfer of wealth from consumers to a producer is a proxy for the social waste generated by 'rent-seeking' and represents a real social cost.[23] Further, the excess profits from monopoly or equivalent restrictions on competition will often exceed the direct distortive costs. That is, rent-seeking is a significant lure and increases the costs of monopoly and regulation substantially.

Box 5 **The economic costs of monopoly and rent-seeking**

A monopolist increases the price above marginal opportunity costs by reducing output. Economists show this through the use of supply and demand schedules. The schedule labelled 'Demand' shows the average willingness to pay of consumers for different units of a good. The lower downward-sloped schedule labelled 'Marginal revenue' (MR) shows how the monopolist's revenue changes with each unit expansion/ reduction in output. If the marginal costs of production are (assumed) constant (shown by the horizontal line labelled 'Supply' = the marginal costs (MC)) then firms in a competitive

---

23 R. A. Posner, 'Social costs of monopoly', *Journal of Political Economy*, 1975, 83: 807–27.

Figure 3 The costs of monopoly

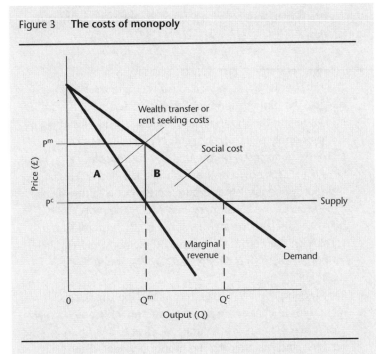

industry produce up to the point where price equals marginal costs, which is at output level Q^c. A monopolist who can influence the price will produce less, and reduce output to Q^m. This is because Q^c does not maximise the monopolist's profits – since the MR schedule is below MC, profits can be increased by reducing output and costs, and increasing price to what the traffic will bear. A monopolist's output (Q^m) is significantly less than the output under competitive conditions (Q^c); and the monopoly price (P^m) higher than the competitive price (P^c). The economic harm or loss created by a monopoly (or legislation that restricts competition) depends on how it was created and sustained:

- **No rent-seeking** – If the monopoly is simply present then the monopoly results in wealth transfer and misallocative effects. The higher monopoly price transfers wealth from consumers to the monopolist. This redistribution is given by the monopoly mark-up above the competitive price (= to marginal costs) on the units of output sold, i.e. $(P^m - P^c) \times Q^m$, shown as the rectangle labelled **A**. This is treated by economists as a pure transfer of wealth which cancels out – the consumers' loss equals the monopolist's gain. The social costs are measured by the lost consumers' surplus on the output not produced owing to the higher monopoly price (the difference $Q^c - Q^m$), shown by the triangle **B**.

- **Rent-seeking** – In a world with rent-seeking the shaded rectangle which was a wealth transfer now becomes a real cost, since it measures the unproductive expenditure in securing and maintaining the monopoly right. The social costs or distortions are now **A + B**. As can be seen, the rent-seeking costs **A** exceed the direct misallocative losses **B** from less output under monopoly by a significant margin. Indeed, under the assumption of constant marginal costs of production, rent-seeking costs can be as much as two times the direct costs of monopoly, i.e. **A = 2B**.

Monopoly may not always be bad. There are several 'justifications' for monopoly – productive efficiency, dynamic efficiency and network effects:

- **Natural monopoly** – Some monopolies can supply the entire market at lower unit costs than two or more competing firms. These are the so-called 'natural monopolies'. Many network or utility industries – or at least their networks of pipes, wires and cables – have this feature.
- **Innovation monopolies** – In industries where product and technical innovation is important, large-scale investment is required to undertake the research and development and the risks of launching new untested products. There is thus active competition among large and small firms to seek out new alternatives and products. A few are successful and grow to be large, even dominant, companies. These monopolies are the outcome of a dynamic competitive process surrounding innovation and generate long-term consumer benefits. The risk is, however, that they acquire market power and exploit consumers by charging high prices, and block competitors. The paradox that monopoly can be competitive was resolved by Joseph Schumpeter over half a century ago.[24] He argued that many would act in a competitive manner because, although dominant in the market, they faced the constant threat of being displaced by firms seeking to develop newer and better products. These 'monopolists', argued Schumpeter, still competed vigorously, not necessarily 'in the market', but 'for the market', i.e. for the right to be the monopolist. This competition places dominant firms under constant pressure from rivals offering better and cheaper products/services seeking to displace them as the sole provider in the marketplace. Thus, the competitive

---

24 J. Schumpeter, *Capitalisation, Democracy and Socialism*, Harper & Row, New York, 1942.

process leads to a regime of *serial* monopolisation of markets consistent with competitive outcomes.

- **Network effects** – A network externality or effect[25] is demand-side externality arising from the interdependence of individual demand. One type is a *direct network effect*, where the value a consumer places on a telephone is directly related to the number of other persons connected to the telephone network. The second is an *indirect network effect*, where demand for a product is related to the number of other people who use the product and the number of complementary products. The latter relates to, say, a computer operating standard where the value of the standard increases when more people and software and applications use the standard. Such network effects mean that large (physical and virtual) networks are more highly valued by consumers, and there is a tendency for these to grow, a situation that may lead to one or a few networks dominating the market. Even though these may have a market power, the existence of one network generates considerable consumer benefits, and by implication the fragmentation of the industry would lead to consumer welfare losses.

Defining legal terms

One area where there was an early interplay between law and economics was in defining key legal terms such as 'relevant market', 'market power' (or dominance, as it is termed under Article 82 of the EC Treaty) and 'effective competition'. Economics

---

25 C. Shapiro and H. R. Varian, *Information Rules – A Strategic Guide to the Network Economy*, Harvard Business School Press, Boston, MA, 1998.

has been used to give these legal terms more precision, and to develop empirical tests to measure them. This has not always been a straightforward exercise, nor one valued by regulators.

The 'relevant market'

Market definition is the cornerstone of any competition law investigation today. To quote one competition regulator, the central issue in assessing a proposed merger was:

> What is the most appropriate definition of the market or markets relevant to the merger taking into account such factors as: whether Scottish salmon is distinct from all other salmon and whether Atlantic salmon from Pacific salmon; the substitutability of other fish for salmon; whether salmon that has been gutted forms a distinct market from salmon that has undergone secondary processing; and the geographic extent of the market or markets.[26]

The importance of whether gutted salmon was in the same market as smoked salmon arises from the way market shares are used in competition law.[27] In EC competition law, as a 'rule of thumb', a firm with 40–50 per cent of a 'relevant market' is deemed dominant, i.e. to have market power, although it is only the abuse of dominance which is illegal. Thus, if the market is defined narrowly, a firm is more likely to be regarded as 'dominant' and attract antitrust scrutiny than if the market is defined widely. This in turn can have a major effect on the outcome of a competition law investigation or court case.

---

26 *Nutreco Holding BV/Norsk Hydro ASA Merger Inquiry Issues Statement*, MMC press release 45/00, 5 September 2000, p. 1.

27 US Supreme Court, 'Market definition generally determines the result of the case', *Eastman Kodak Co. v Image Technical Services Inc*. 504 US 451, 469 n. 15 (1992).

The concept of a relevant market (in EC law) or antitrust market (in US law) is, however, a legal construct. It arose from the rather commonsense ruling of the US courts in the late 1940s that in order for market power to be present, there must be a market.[28] And as is the case in litigation where there is a concept and a claim by one side, there will be a dispute as to its validity by the other. Hence, as the case law developed, there were different formulations and legal applications to specific facts which lacked rigour. Indeed, the situation in the USA was described by Donald Turner as 'a bloody mess'.[29]

The position was not much better in Europe. The European courts set down the test for a market in terms of the notion of 'sufficient substitutes' or 'interchangeability'. In *Continental Can*, a leading EC case on the matter, the European Court stated that a market was defined by: '… those characteristics of the products in question by virtue of which they are particularly apt to satisfy an inelastic need and are only to a limited extent interchangeable with other products'.[30]

In *United Brands*, where the applicant argued that bananas were in the same market as other fruit, the European Court said that this depended on whether a banana could be: '… singled out by such special features distinguishing it from other fruits that it is only to a limited extent interchangeable with them and is only

---

28 *United States v Columbia Steel Co.* 334 US 496 (1948).

29 D. F. Turner, 'The role of the "market concept" in antitrust law', *Antitrust Law Journal*, 1980, 49: 1150.

30 The test of 'sufficient substitutes' or interchangeability was first set out by the EJC in Case 6/72, *Europemballage and Continental Can v Commission* [1973] ECR 215, para. 32, and *Hoffman-La Roche & Co. AG v Commission* [1978] ECR 461, para. 23.

exposed to their competition in a way that is hardly perceptible'.[31] That is, a market was to be determined by the softness and chewability of different fruits, so that toothless consumers (the old and infirm) constituted a separate relevant market from those who bought hard apples. This was hardly economics!

Economists for their part did not define markets.[32] Most economics textbooks assumed rather than established the existence of a market. The early chapters would define a market as an arena – or, to use a more contemporary word, a 'space' – where homogeneous products are exchanged at a uniform price. Thus, product homogeneity and price uniformity seemed key aspects of market definition (often referred to misleadingly as 'the law of one price'). A firm in a competitive market faced infinitely elastic demand at the prevailing price, which in plain language meant it did not have the ability to determine prices. That is, a firm in a competitive market is a price-taker, not a price-maker (or price-fixer). The economists' approach was not about market definition as such, but market power, i.e. the ability of firms to profitably raise prices above competitive levels.

Indeed, some economists are hostile to the market definition approach, but this is greatly overstated – the criticism ignores real-world data problems that prevent elasticities and other indices of market power being directly estimated, and the fact that

---

31 *United Brands v Commission* Case 27/76 [1978] ECR 207; [1978] 1 CMLR 429, para. 22.

32 In 1982 George Stigler declared: 'My lament is that this battle on market definition ... has received virtually no attention from us economists. Except for a casual flirtation with cross elasticities of demand and supply, the determination of markets has remained an undeveloped area of economic research at either the theoretical or empirical level'; G. Stigler, 'The economist and the problem of monopoly', *American Economic Review*, 1982, 72: 1–11.

today competition authorities do not mechanically apply market definition (it is only a tool to assist in identifying market power).

Notwithstanding this, given the judicial requirement for market definition, economists responded by applying their analytical toolkit to assist the courts and regulators to define relevant product markets more rigorously. The EC Notice on market definition was significant in this regard by setting out an economic test for market definition. It suggested that the Hypothetical Monopolist Test (HMT) or SSNIP (an acronym for 'Small but Significant Non-transitory Increase in Price') test be used to define a relevant product (and geographical) market. The SSNIP test establishes the type and range of products over which a hypothetical monopolist of a single or group of products under consideration would find it profitable to raise price 5 or 10 per cent above the competitive price (Box 5).

While the hypothetical nature of the test suggests to some that it is of little practical use, and indeed it is described officially as only one way to define a market and as a 'thought experiment', economists have developed techniques and empirical tests to assist regulators and courts to undertake a more fact-based approach to market definition and market-power assessment. Today, economists routinely assist companies, their legal advisers and regulators to define relevant product and geographical markets.

Effective competition

The legal goal of EC competition law is to maintain 'effective competition'. Yet in practice there are two problems with this goal – it is undefined and ambiguous.

Box 6 **Pizza – a ssnip at the price?**

'Those who regard pizza as a staple diet item would be deeply concerned with recent reports that "Pizzas cost more dough" following the acquisition of Eagle Boys pizza chain by Pizza Hut. ... Before contemplating a class action by pizza aficionados forced to stomach the new prices, it is perhaps useful to apply some simple competition analysis.

'The ssnip test poses the question – what would happen to the quantity of pizza demanded if a hypothetical monopolist controlling all supply of pizza increased the price by such a ssnip. Generally a ssnip of five percent lasting for at least one year is examined. Would enough pizza eaters switch to other products to satisfy their need for a fast food fix so that the price increase was unprofitable? If so then the market against which the pizza company merger should be tested is wider than just pizza. One would have to draw a wider market including perhaps fish and chips, burgers or other types of fast food. That wider market would then be given a ssnip test to see if perhaps something at home might be a reasonable substitute. If however a ssnip could be imposed without sufficient customers switching, then pizza is more likely to comprise a market on its own right.

'... the [New Zealand Commerce] Commission concluded that Pizza Hut, after it acquired Eagle Boys, would still face sufficient competition from a combination of other pizza suppliers, other fast food types and potential new entrants, that it would not gain market dominance.'[33]

---

33   *New Zealand Institute of Economic Research – Update*, September 2000.

The term 'effective competition' is not defined in law. Moreover there are considerable differences of opinion as to the meaning of 'effective competition' and when it is being violated – in theory, fact and law.

Most contemporary competition law textbooks begin by observing that competition can be defined in a number of different ways as: 1) rivalry, 2) the absence of market power, 3) an outcome or condition in the market where individual firms or buyers do not have influence over price, 4) an atomistic market structure, and/or 5) a state of affairs where consumer welfare cannot be further improved. To this should be added the Hayekian (Austrian economics) view of competition as a 'discovery process', and the Schumpeterian view of competition as a dynamic innovative process (see above).

Lawyers and regulators have traditionally ignored these and moved on rapidly to a discussion of the decisions and cases. Yet without a theory of effective competition it is hard to identify it in practice, to frame and apply laws, and more importantly to identify and quantify anticompetitive harm. The rise of the economic approach has redressed the current vagueness in the law by endorsing consumer welfare as the benchmark. This has not been the way competition law has been applied, however, and even with the current reforms there are still large pockets where the law takes a different tack.

EC competition law has operated with an overly structural view of competition based on a mix of the workable competition concept developed in the 1930/40s with the German Freiberg School 'Ördo Liberal' view of intervention as primarily designed to reduce the economic power of firms and organisations in the economy. This translated into theories and intervention that equated 'harm to competitors' as 'harm to competition'. The European Commission was frequently criticised for using competition law to protect competitors rather than competition by blocking mergers that gave a large entity an advantage over its competitors irrespective of the likely consumer benefits.

These differing views of competition came into sharp relief in the controversy surrounding the treatment by the European Commission of the GE/Honeywell merger.[34] This was what competition practitioners call a 'conglomerate merger'. A conglomerate merger is one between two firms that each produce a different range of products – for example, one produces large aircraft engines and the other avionics (as was the case in GE/ Honeywell), or between two consumer goods companies each producing distinct product ranges. The European Commission blocked the merger between General Electric and Honeywell using a theory of competitive harm based on 'portfolio effects' or 'range effects'. A merger that generated advantages, such as a larger product range, greater efficiencies, lower prices, new products or a better distribution system, was seen to entrench and enhance a firm's dominance, and to give it anti-competitive advantages irrespective of the possible consumer benefits. The US antitrust authorities, however, cleared the same merger, and not only dismissed the validity of the portfolio effects theory, but saw such combinations as generating consumer benefits, not harm.

While the European Commission sought to portray the difference as one of degree, the US antitrust officials were having nothing of it. The then US Assistant Attorney General for Antitrust described it as a 'rather fundamental doctrinal disagreement over

---

34 C. G. Veljanovski, 'EC merger policy after GE/Honeywell and Airtours', *Antitrust Bulletin*, 2004, 49: 153–93.

the economic purpose and scope of antitrust enforcement. ... In sum, we appear to disagree over the meaning of competition'.[35] A later analysis by the US Department of Justice (which is responsible for the enforcement of US antitrust laws) stated:

> In summary, we found no factual support for any of the key elements of the range effects theories of competitive harm with respect to the GE/Honeywell merger. To the contrary, we concluded that to the extent those theories were based on the argument that the merged firm would have the ability and incentive to offer customers lower prices and better products, that meant the merger should benefit customers both directly – through the lower prices and better products offered by the merged firm – and indirectly – by inducing rivals to respond with their own lower prices and product improvements. That, in our view, was a reason to welcome the merger, not condemn it[36]

It went on to comment, in line with the general reaction of European judges rejecting the European Commission's economic analysis, that 'without a high standard of proof, range effects theory runs the risk of becoming an ill-defined, catch-all theory that allows antitrust regulators to challenge virtually any merger on the basis of vague fears of "dominance"'. Interestingly, GE's appeal against the European Commission, although it failed, still saw the court reject not the theory of 'portfolio effects' (which remains part of EC jurisprudence) but the fact that the European

---

35 C. A. James, 'Reconciling divergent enforcement policies: where do we go from here?', Fordham Corporate Law Institute 28th Annual Conference on International Law and Policy, New York, 25 October 2001.

36 'DOJ Antitrust Division submission for OECD Roundtable on Portfolio Effects in Conglomerate Mergers and Range Effects: The United States perspective', *OECD Symposium on Portfolio Effects in Conglomerate Mergers*, OECD, Paris, 2002.

Commission had failed to convincingly establish on the facts that the merged entity would behave in an anti-competitive manner.[37] Again, the European Commission had over-relied on theory and presumption.

The view that competitor harm is the economic and legal test triggering legal intervention is felt in other important areas of European antitrust law. For example, the European Commission, confirmed by the courts in *Tetra Laval*, have applied the concept of (what I call) 'leveraged dominance'. This is where a firm that has market power in one market is seen as having the ability to leverage (that is apply) that market power into other related markets where it does not have a dominant position. The US courts have taken the view that it is not unlawful for a firm dominant in one market to use its market power to gain a competitive advantage in neighbouring markets, unless this either protects its existing monopoly or creates a dangerous probability of gaining a monopoly in the adjacent market.[38] In Europe the concept of leveraged dominance appears a fixed feature of antitrust law.

Another area where competitor harm dominates the European Commission's thinking is in its treatment of loyalty and fidelity rebates. These are discounts given to sales agents and distributors based on the volume of sales. Take the case of British Airways' use of rebates to reward travel agents for meeting sales targets in the late 1990s. Virgin formally complained about this practice to both the European Commission and the US antitrust authorities. The European Commission held that it was anti-competitive,[39] whereas

---

37 Case T-210-01, *General Electric v Commission* (2006).
38 *Antitrust Developments*, 4th edn, American Bar Association, Chicago, 1997, pp. 282–5.
39 Case IV/D-2/34.780, *Virgin/British Airways* (1999).

when Virgin sued BA using the same theory in the US, the claim was rejected.[40] In the USA such discounts are seen as benefiting consumers and are rarely successfully challenged as long as they are not predatory.

It should be noted that the great danger of the European Commission's past approach is that it enables antitrust and merger laws to be used strategically by rivals to block competition. Indeed, many competition authorities are over-reliant on complaints and evidence assembled by competitors, and this has the effect of skewing antitrust enforcement towards competitors' concerns rather than preventing consumer harm. Indeed, the strategic use of antitrust to block competition is a real concern. A frequent criticism of US antitrust litigation, where plaintiffs can be awarded treble damages, is that it allows firms to hold their otherwise legitimate competitors to ransom. In 2006 the chief executive of the UK Office of Fair Trading (John Fingleton) criticised the UK appeal process through the Competition Appeal Tribunal for allowing competitors to delay and block otherwise 'efficient' mergers.

Efficiency: goal, defence or offence?

The economic approach emphasises the importance of efficient law and efficiency. Yet efficiency plays an uncertain and ambiguous role in competition law. Efficiency concerns have been present and are now explicitly taken into account in Article 81 covering anti-competitive agreements.[41] This is because the market share thresholds are set at lower levels, and there is greater danger of

---

40 *Virgin Atlantic Airways Ltd v British Airways PLC* 257 F.3d 256 (2d Cir. 2001).
41 EC *Guidelines on the Application of Article 81(3) of the Treaty*, 2004/C 101/08.

confusing contractual restrictions with restricting competition. In this area EC law has moved more squarely to what is called a 'rule of reason' approach, comparing the restrictive effects with the commercial and economic benefits. On the other hand there are no merger laws, with the exception of Canada's, that use an efficiency standard to evaluate mergers. Most merger laws seek to maximise consumer welfare and either ignore efficiencies, give them little weight and/or take them into account only to the extent that the likely gains are shared with consumers.[42]

This agnosticism contrasts with economic theory. Oliver Williamson, when an economist at the US Department of Justice, was asked to consider this question and came up with a simple yet powerful analysis of the interplay between (marginal) cost efficiencies and consumer welfare.[43] Williamson concluded that 'a merger which yields nontrivial real marginal cost economies must produce substantial market power and result in relatively large price increases for the net allocative effects to be negative'. To illustrate using simplifying assumptions – if a firm's marginal costs fell by 5 to 10 per cent, price increases of the order of 20 to 40 per cent would be required to wipe out the economic benefits. While the implications for practical antitrust policy were cautiously drawn by Williamson, the analysis strongly suggested that the enforcement authorities should take evidence of cost efficiencies

---

42   The difference in approach is that the consumer welfare model focuses on maximising consumers' surplus, while the efficiency or total surplus maximises both consumers' and producers' surplus. This implies that a reorientation of competition law based on a consumer welfare model overshoots the efficiency theory of competition law, and implicitly reflects a distributional bias in favour of consumers and against firms.

43   O. E. Williamson, 'Economies as an antitrust defense: the welfare trade-offs', *American Economic Review*, 1968, LVIII: 18–36.

seriously, and contemplate the possibility of a welfare or competition efficiency trade-off.

In practice, the claim that a merger will generate significant efficiencies is often treated sceptically because they have been easy to claim but hard to establish, and empirical research has generally failed to identify large post-merger efficiency gains. Indeed, the old EC Merger Regulation did not permit economic efficiency factors to override competition concerns because of pressure from the UK government, which feared that an efficiency defence would be used by the European Commission to subvert competition law in favour of old-style industrial policy.

The European Commission's treatment of efficiencies went one step too far by occasionally treating them as anti-competitive. This again was the result of its reliance on a 'theory' of competitor harm rather than consumer harm or an efficiency standard. In several prominent cases the European Commission appeared to be concluding that a merger that generated productive efficiencies would give the larger merged entity advantages over its competitors, and that these advantages would enhance its dominant position. Thus, instead of there being an efficiency defence, the Commission was seen to have created an 'efficiency offence'. For example in *AT&T/NCR*[44] the parties' claims that costs savings would arise from complementarities between technical know-how and the marketing of workstations was treated as evidence that the merging parties would be able to drive rivals out of the market. Fortunately, the new EC Merger Regulation recognises the scope for efficiency in merger clearance and rids the law of the 'efficiency offence'. But it does not

---

44   OJ 1991 C16/20.

create an efficiency standard for merger clearance. In line with other merger laws, efficiencies have to be established and shared with consumers.

Antitrust and the new economy

The so-called 'new economy' posed another challenge to antitrust enforcement, economics and indeed the business sector. One need not be reminded of the dot.com bubble and the 'irrational exuberance' of the late 1990s. The economic approach has not been immune from the confusion and exaggeration that characterised the period. This has been particularly the case in 'high-tech' industries where recent developments in economic theory have suggested new grounds for intervention that have divided economists and lawyers,[45] while this time uniting EU and US competition authorities.

The battle of theories

Decisions and statements by the European Commission in the late 1990s suggested that competition rules would be more stringently applied to the new economy. As the then European Competition Commissioner (Mario Monti) stated: '... even if the pace of high technology sectors means that market failures last only for a short time – and I have serious doubts about this – this does not mean that we should be less concerned'.[46]

---

45 C. Veljanovski, 'EC antitrust in the new economy – is the European Commission's view of the network economy right?', *European Competition Law Review*, 2001, 22: 115–21.

46 M. Monti, 'Competition and information technologies', address to Kangaroo Group, Brussels, 18 September 2000.

This was more or less the position taken by the US antitrust authorities. Given the rapid, innovative, immature and dynamic nature of these sectors, this approach attracted criticism. This is because one associates monopoly concerns with entrenched mature industries, and not dynamic and innovative sectors, often sustaining huge investments and losses, and in the initial stages of development and growth. *The Economist* magazine's reaction was to declare 'antitrust run amok?', arguing that the best approach was forbearance:

> … too often their [the antitrust authorities] approach relies on their own predictions of how the market will evolve or, worse, on the assumption that it will not. This despite the fact that technology has become the sledgehammer to once formidable barriers to entry. …
>
> The 'new economy' is also allowing trust-busters to let their imagination run riot. Technological change creates particularly tricky problems for antitrust. As Larry Summers, America's treasury secretary, pointed out recently, innovation is increasingly driven by firms that win temporary monopoly power but enjoy it for a moment before being replaced by a company with a better product which itself gains a short-lived monopoly. This suggests that the new economy may feature more monopolies than the old, but few of them will harm consumers; on the contrary, if this dynamic encourages innovation, consumers can benefit. And this implies that trust-busters would often do best to leave well alone, unless and until it becomes clear that a monopoly is not temporary and that it is being exploited not to encourage but inhibit innovation – as in the Microsoft case.[47]

---

47   'Trust and antitrust', *The Economist*, 7 October 2000, p. 21.

The new-economy industries are characterised by technological change and product innovation. They also have some peculiarities arising from the technology used, and the demand for communications services. Important among these are network effects (see above). In the late 1990s the European Commission adopted an extreme version of network effects theory. It began with the empirical but untested premise that the communications sector harbours pervasive and significant network effects.[48] These demand-side economies of scale generate positive feedback effects ('success breeds success') as more subscribers/customers join a network, ultimately tipping the market ('snowballing it') so that one network/standard/product dominates. Consumers become locked into the network/product. As a result, even networks offering superior services cannot dislodge the larger network. Indeed, there is a path dependence which can see early developers (first mover advantages) becoming dominant by capturing new growth so that the economy may adopt an inefficient solution. In short, the structural features of the new economy impel it to monopoly and inefficiency. This, in turn, argued the Commission, justified vigorous antitrust enforcement (and additional sectoral regulation).

The alternative approach takes a more benign view of network effects. It regards the monopoly concerns as a misreading of the economics and history of innovation, and as ignoring the massive consumer benefits arising from network growth driven by network effects. Second, tipping and monopoly abuse depend

---

48 H. Ungerer, 'Access issues under EU regulation and anti-trust law – the case of telecommunications and Internet markets', Panel on Substantive Comparative Antitrust Issues in Japan, the US and the European Union, Washington, DC, 23/24 June 2000, p. 4.

not on the mere existence of network effects but on a number of stringent assumptions; foremost among these is that the networks are not interconnected. Further, the choice of network effects theory significantly affects the treatment of the facts. Under the European Commission's view many facts will be treated as evidence of monopolistic abuses that under the milder version are pro-competitive. High profit margins might appear to be benign and necessary to recover legitimate investment returns in a Schumpeterian framework; or alternatively they are seen as evidence of consumer exploitation and monopoly power. Market dominance in the former case is likely to be temporary, but in the latter to be seen as entrenched. Aggressive pricing that looks predatory in a conventional market might constitute a rational competitive strategy in a market where one's future existence depends on early penetration. The standard approach may result in excessively narrow product market definitions and too much regulatory intervention, which may chill investment and stall innovation.[49] Under a Schumpeterian view market definition should use a wide lens to take into account longer-term non-price factors.[50]

---

49 A study of 21 major industries in the USA covering the period 1947–91 found that each antitrust filing was associated with a significant decline in investment in the respective industry; G. Bittlingmayer, 'Regulatory uncertainty and investment: evidence from antitrust enforcement', *Cato Journal*, 2001, 20: 295–325.

50 This view was given a boost in 1995 when the then US Assistant Attorney General for Antitrust argued that standard market definition approach was flawed in innovative industries; R. Gilbert and S. Sunshine, 'Incorporating dynamic efficiency concerns in merger analysis – the use of innovation markets', *Antitrust Law Journal*, 1995, 63: 569–602. Also OFT/Oftel, *Innovation and Competition Policy*, Economics Discussion Paper, 2002; W. J. Baumol, *The Free Market Innovation Machine*, Princeton University Press, Princeton, NJ, 2002.

EC new-economy merger decisions

The European Commission applied its version of network effects theory to several mergers in the late 1990s/early 2000s.[51] One was Vodafone's hostile, and then friendly, takeover of Mannesmann.[52] The proposed merger would (and did) create the largest pan-European mobile network operator. Vodafone also claimed that as one of the benefits of the merger it would create (innovate) a seamless pan-European mobile service, instead of the existing method of international roaming agreements between separately owned national networks. The European Commission was concerned by the large expansion in Vodafone's geographical footprint and customer base, and its potential ability to 'leverage' its 'dominant' position in the provision of the 'seamless pan-European mobile service to corporate customers'. It argued that Vodafone would secure a 'first mover advantage' which other operators could not replicate:

> The merged entity would be the only mobile operator able
> to capture future growth through new customers, because
> new customers would be attracted by the services offered
> by Vodafone AirTouch/Mannesmann on its own network.
> Given their inability to replicate the new entity's network,
> competitors will have at best, i.e. if they are allowed
> access to Vodafone's network at all, significant costs and
> performance/quality disadvantages given their dependency
> on Vodafone AirTouch/Mannesmann, for instance on
> roaming agreements in order to offer 'equivalent' pan-
> European mobile services. This situation is likely to

---

51 Case IV/M.1069, *WorldCom/MCI* (1998); Case COMP/M.1439, *Telia/Telenor* (1999); Case COMP/M.1795, *Vodafone AirTouch/Mannesmann* (2000); Case COMP/JV.48, *Vodafone/Vivendi/Canal+* (2000); Case COMP/M.1741, *MCI-WorldCom/Sprint* (2002).

52 Case COMP/M.1795, *Vodafone AirTouch/Mannesmann* (2000).

> entrench the merged entity into a dominant position on the
> emerging pan-European market for international mobile
> customers for the foreseeable future because customers of
> other operators would generally prefer the merged entity
> to other mobile operators given its unrivalled possibility to
> provide advanced seamless services across Europe.[53]

The European Commission's reasoning and 'factual' analyses were flawed on a number of counts. First, it relied on theory and assumption, rather than a credible fact-based analysis of whether the feared anti-competitive outcomes were likely to happen. It is highly likely that had Vodafone challenged the Commission's analysis, from what we know today, it would not have satisfied the burden of proof now required by the courts in merger analysis. Vodafone did not have a dominant position in any national mobile market, and was with one exception not the largest mobile operator in the countries in which it was present. But more to the legal point, the proposed merger did not create or enhance a dominant position in any relevant existing product or geographical market. The European Commission, in effect, based its intervention on the tautological claim that should the new product be successfully launched, the merged entity would be dominant in the supply of that product. Third, while the European Commission claimed that Vodafone's coverage could not be replicated, no sooner had the ink dried on its merger decision than other mobile operators began to acquire national networks (such as France Telecom) to develop pan-European networks. Finally, Vodafone, perhaps as a result of the undertakings it was required to give the Commission to get the merger

---

53   *Vodafone/Mannesmann*, para. 45.

cleared, never introduced the new product, nor have its competitors ever sought access to Vodafone's network using the undertakings (which it is rumoured were drafted for the European Commission by a rival operator seeking to inhibit Vodafone's expansion).

The European Commission's subsequent decision in *Vodafone/Vivendi-Canal+*[54] showed an even more speculative use of economics. This was a 50-50 joint venture to develop a branded horizontal multi-access Internet portal (Vizzavi) across Europe, which would provide customers with a seamless range of Web-based interactive services. Vodafone was to supply the mobile service in ten EU member states; Vivendi the content. As a result of the proposed joint venture there would have been no increased concentration, no horizontal market concerns, and no finding that Vodafone was dominant in any relevant market. The Commission's concern was that Vodafone's size combined with Vivendi's content could lead 'to the creation or strengthening of a dominant position in an emerging pan-European market for WAP-based mobile Internet access'[55] by leveraging the company's large customer base in national markets for mobile telephony into the market for mobile Internet access. Similar arguments were used to justify concerns over the market for horizontal portals, although the Commission accepted that 'the Parties individually do not at present enjoy significant market share on the horizontal portals market'. It argued, however, that Vodafone and Vivendi-Canal+ might be able to extend their position of dominance in pay TV and 'market power' (but not dominance) in mobiles into national markets for horizontal portals. Moreover, the Commission found

---

54 Case COMP/JV.48, *Vodafone/Vivendi/Canal+* (2000).

55 *Vodafone/Vivendi/Canal+*, para. 68.

that the joint venture might lead to or strengthen a 'dominant position' in the 'WAP-roaming based pan-European portal market using ubiquitous pan-European mobile telecommunications services'; a market that did not yet exist. Again the facts did not support the Commission's analysis. WAP did not take off, the dot.com bubble burst, and the Vizzavi joint venture folded several years later.

The danger of 'nip and tuck' economics

As the preceding examples show, economics can be used to develop antitrust doctrine based solely on theoretical concerns that have not been tested by the regulator (or economists) and which at best have questionable empirical relevance. What is remarkable about these decisions is the way the European Commission used this new economic theory to evolve legal enforcement decisions. Further, these decisions treated innovation as a competition problem, and equated 'first mover advantage' with dominance. Clearly no acceptance of Schumpeterian competition here!

These examples also sound a more cautionary note to the application of economics in law. In the last decade or so there has been a movement to develop more realistic economic theories of competitive and anti-competitive practices and behaviour. These draw heavily on game theory, switching costs, asymmetric information, or what Coase identified as transactions costs. But instead of finding that markets economise on these to develop efficient responses, this literature finds the opposite – the tendency of a few larger firms to take advantage of these frictions to harm their rivals and raise their costs through pricing, investment, and contractual and strategic actions.[56] Ronald Cass and Keith Hylton[57] have gone farther, calling this the 'nip and tuck' school of antitrust economics, which finds:

> ... reasons why seemingly innocent – or at least ordinary – business activity actually could be designed to subvert competitors and, perhaps, competition. Writings in this genre deploy sophisticated arguments to establish that conduct that looks ambiguous or even benign should be treated as contrary to the antitrust law's constraints. These writings frequently rely on subtle distinctions to separate the conduct they find pro-competitive and advocate antitrust remedies that assertedly do, if not perfect justice, its next of kin. These writings also typically rely on complex mathematical or game-theoretic models to demonstrate that important aspects of ordinary market competition can break down under certain assumptions (assumptions that are difficult, if not impossible, to verify from observable data).

While these models have enriched our understanding of the competitive process, they raise concerns that theory, albeit more complex theory, is mistaken for reality.

Assessment

The current rise of the economic approach has put EC competition on a solid and more rational footing. As has been shown, however,

56 This branch of the literature was launched by S. C. Salop and D. Sheffman, 'Raising rivals' costs', *American Economic Review*, 1983, 73: 267–71.

57 R. A. Cass and K. N. Hylton, 'Preserving competition: economic analysis, legal standards and Microsoft', *George Mason Law Review*, 1999, 8: 36–9. Also F. M. Fisher, 'Games economists play: a noncooperative view', *Rand Journal of Economics*, 1989, 20: 113–24.

economics can be both used and abused; and theory can substitute for fact and common sense. Remarkably, or perhaps paradoxically, after decades of the formalistic application of competition law and the adoption of some economics, we have judges to thank for not only ensuring the rightful place of the economic approach in competition law but also for forcing regulators to combine good economics with good evidence. This surely has been one of the most interesting, unexpected and subtle examples of the interplay between economics and law in recent times.

7 REGULATION

Regulation is on the rise. We have never been richer or more regulated.[1] Taking the UK alone, it has been calculated that in 2004 there were 358 volumes of public statutes, 682 volumes of other statutes and many more of statutory instruments, which together took up over 100 shelves in the British Library. This growing mountain of statutory law (regulation) has been described 'as beyond the average citizen's pocket to purchase, beyond his book-shelves to accommodate, beyond his leisure to study and beyond his intellect to comprehend'.[2]

Both the Margaret Thatcher and Tony Blair governments in the UK have been concerned about the growth of regulation. The Thatcher-era White Papers were full of concerns about the need to avoid the excesses of so-called 'US-style regulation' – cost-plus litigious regulation which places excessive burdens on industry and the consumer. The Blair government, and now the EU Commission, has increasingly expressed concerns about regulation and 'red tape' burdening business, and reducing economic growth and productivity. Indeed, regulatory reform has been

1   A. Schleifer, 'Understanding regulation', *European Financial Management*, 2005, 11: 439–51; E. L. Glaeser and A. Schleifer, 'The rise of the regulatory state', *Journal of Economic Literature*, 2003, 41: 401–25.
2   Sir Cecil Carr, when chairman of the Statute Law Committee, quoted in N. Cawthorne, *The Strange Laws of Old England*, Piatkus, London, 2004, p. 1.

put high on the political agenda, so much so that at the 2005 British general election the two main parties vied with each other over the costs savings they could make from cutting waste in government and reducing the regulatory burden, with the Blair government committed to a £10 billion saving in the burden of regulation.

Despite these concerns and efforts, regulation and its detail and complexity have grown unabated. During Margaret Thatcher's governments major supply-side reforms (liberalisation, privatisation and deregulation) led to the increasing use of regulation administered by semi-autonomous public bodies.[3] These supply-side reforms spread across Europe. But they have led to an inevitable paradox – as private ownership replaced state ownership, state regulation grew massively. Much of this regulation had a strong justification in controlling the newly privatised utilities' market power. A privately owned gas or electricity company cannot be set free to charge its customers what it likes, and to prevent others from competing.[4] Economic regulation, first in the form of price controls and the dismantling of barriers to entry (liberalisation), and later access and structural reforms, has grown substantially in depth and sophistication. Indeed, in some areas the pace of regulatory reform has led to a 'regulatory incontinence' – a continuous process of review, revision and

3   See C. G. Veljanovski, *Selling the State – Privatisation in Britain*, Weidenfeld & Nicolson, London, 1988; C. G. Veljanovski (ed.), *Privatisation and Competition – a Market Prospectus*, IEA, London, 1989.

4   C. G. Veljanovski (ed.), *Regulation and the Market – an Assessment of the Growth of Regulation in the UK*, IEA, London, 1991; C. G. Veljanovski, *The Future of Industry Regulation in the UK*, European Policy Forum, London, 1993; J. Flemming (chair), *The Report of the Commission on the Regulation of Utilities*, Hansard Society/European Policy Forum, London, 1996.

re-regulation with attendant high transactions costs and regulatory uncertainty.

Growth has also taken place in so-called social regulation – labour (social charter, sex and racial discrimination, unfair dismissal), product, environmental and human rights regulation.[5] This type of regulation is not new, and historically marked the beginning of state intervention and the welfare state.

The economic approach is playing an increasing role in guiding and criticising the reforms of economic and social regulation.

Models of regulation

The nature, growth and effects of regulation within and across countries are the outcome of the interaction between politics, economics and law – a volatile cocktail by any measure. This has made it difficult to adequately model regulation because often its goals are multi-faceted, it is multi-layered, and is the outcome of legislative, political and bureaucratic actions, and its effects are poorly understood and hard to measure.

Market failures framework

The normative economic theory of regulation was and still is largely based on the market failures framework. This views regulation as promoting the public interest (efficiency), and government as organising the production of public goods, such as defence, law and order, and other products and services that cannot be supplied by the marketplace. As already discussed, it uses the

5   W. K. Viscusi, J. E. Harrington and J. M. Vernon, *Economics of Regulation and Antitrust*, 4th edn, MIT Press, Cambridge, MA, 2005; A. I. Ogus (ed.), *Regulation, Economics and the Law*, Edward Elgar, Cheltenham, 2001.

perfectly competitive market model as the policy benchmark. Any departure from the conditions of perfect competition indicates market failure. The rationale for regulation is to remedy various kinds of market failure. The most prominent market failures are externalities (external or social costs), market power and inadequate information. The limitation of this approach has already been discussed in relation to Coase's analysis.

The problem arises when the market failure approach is used to provide an explanation (positive theory) of regulation and government behaviour. For example, one survey by two British economists claimed that: 'The normal pattern is that market failure provides the rationale for the introduction of regulation, but the scope of regulation is then extended to a wide range of matters which are the subject of general or sectional interests, regardless of whether there is any element of market failure or not.'[6]

While this pattern is discernible, the 'it all began to deal with market failure but then went wrong' thesis does not explain why this occurs. As Stigler has commented, if this is the economist's approach to regulation, then a 'theory of errors' is required to understand the regulatory process. Indeed, Stigler has argued that economists commit many errors but their most frequent one is to believe other economists.

An alternative view is that much regulation has little to do with market failure from inception, and that the suggested pattern above is not a mistake. The emerging consensus among US economists in the 1980s was that regulation invariably caused rather than responded to market failure:

6   J. Kay and J. Vickers, 'Regulatory reform in Britain', *Economic Policy*, 1988, 7: 334.

By the early 1970s the overwhelming majority of economists had reached consensus on two points. First, economic regulation did not succeed in protecting consumers against monopolies, and indeed often served to create monopolies out of workably competitive industries or to protect monopolies against new firms seeking to challenge their position. Second, in circumstances where market failures were of enduring importance (such as environmental protection), traditional standard-setting regulation was usually a far less effective remedy than the use of markets and incentives (such as emissions taxes or tradable emissions permits).[7]

In Europe the reasons for regulation were more ideological under the sway of the 'mixed economy', socialism and indeed communism, if one includes central and eastern Europe. Thus the intervention of the state went farther than would be conceivable in the USA. Many industries were state-owned and were captured by their managers, workers and politicians. In Europe the crises came first in the failure of these state-owned enterprises, and, with their privatisation, concerns over the design and effectiveness of their regulation, and the accountability of the new regulatory agencies.[8]

Positive theory of regulation

The positive theory of regulation, while not disagreeing that regulation should be in the public interest, finds this an inadequate explanation of regulation as it is. Rather, it applies the economist's conceptual framework to model regulation to generate predictions

---

7   R. G. Noll, 'Regulation after Reagan', *Regulation*, 1988, 3: 20.
8   C. Graham, 'Is there a crisis in regulatory accountability?', in R. Baldwin, et al. (eds), *A Reader on Regulation*, Oxford University Press, Oxford, 1998.

of its form and effects in practice. It finds that often regulation is 'deliberately inefficient' in response to the forces of demand and supply in the political market for legislation. Or, put more prosaically, regulation is often 'efficient' in achieving predictably inefficient redistributions of wealth in favour of interest groups.

Regulation creates winners and losers. While society at large may be interested in efficient regulation which maximises wealth irrespective of who gains and loses, in practice these redistributive effects will have an important influence on political support and opposition to different regulatory proposals. It would be contrary to the economist's postulate of self-interested behaviour to assume that individuals, interest groups and politicians are oblivious to the way regulation affects their welfare. The losers may have something to say about 'efficient' regulation that harms their interests and wealth, and be sufficiently encouraged to oppose it; and likewise those favoured by regulation may lobby for such legislation even if it is inefficient. That is, the economist's theory of maximising behaviour might give rise to a positive theory of regulation which is more driven by distributional than efficiency concerns.

George Stigler was the first to provide such a positive theory of regulation. He took the position that regulation was motivated by its distributional effects, pandering to sectional interests from inception and not as an afterthought: 'The paramount role traditionally assigned by economists to government regulation was to correct the failures of the private market (the unconsidered effects of behaviour on outsiders), but in fact the premier role of modern regulation is to redistribute income.'[9]

---

9   G. J. Stigler (ed.), *Chicago Studies in Political Economy*, University of Chicago Press, Chicago, 1988, p. xii.

Subsequent research does not generate the strong conclusions of Stigler's initial model.[10] After all, if 'capture' and shifting wealth to politically effective industry and special interest groups are the engines of modern regulation, then it is hard to explain why deregulation and privatisation occurred.[11]

The distinctive feature of the positive theory of regulation is that it applies the market concepts of supply and demand to the political or legislative marketplace to explain political and regulatory processes and outcomes. The primary 'product' being transacted in this political marketplace is seen as wealth transfers. The demand for legislation comes from cohesive coordinated groups, typically industry or special interest groups, and hence differs from the real marketplace, where all consumers are represented. The supply side of legislation is less easy to define given the nature of the political and legislative processes. The state, however, has a monopoly over one basic resource: the power to legitimately coerce. This leads to the view that because the legislative process is skewed to the benefit of cohesive groups that can lobby effectively, it tends to be captured, or to overly pander to special interest groups. Indeed, this gave rise to a pessimistic assessment of the sustainability of a liberal and open society as politics and government became overwhelmed by special interest politics that undermine economic growth and social progress.[12]

---

10   R. Posner, 'Theories of economic regulation', *Bell Journal of Economics and Management Science*, 1974, 5: 22–50; S. Peltzman, 'Toward a more general theory of regulation', *Journal of Law and Economics*, 1976, 19: 211–40; G. Becker, 'A theory of competition among pressure groups for political influence', *Quarterly Journal of Economics*, 1983, 98: 371–400.

11   S. Peltzman, 'The economic theory of regulation after a decade of deregulation', *Brookings Papers on Economic Activity – Microeconomics*, Brookings Institution, Washington, DC, 1989, pp. 1–59.

12   M. Olson, *The Rise and Decline of Nations*, Yale University Press, New Haven, CT, 1982.

Not only can regulation have misallocative effects but it gives rise to what might be called a *transactions costs economy*. As noted earlier, public choice economists have coined the term rent-seeking to describe unproductive profit-seeking by special interest groups to secure favourable legislation designed to increase their wealth. Legislation that creates barriers to competition or confers monopoly rights increases the wealth of those favoured, which cannot be eroded or competed away.

Juxtaposed against the wealth-redistributive effects of statutory law is the alleged efficiency of the common law. A number of theories have been advanced that the common law was, and perhaps still is, guided by efficiency considerations either because of the constraints on judicial decision-making and its immunity from 'politics', or as the unintended outcome of the efforts of private litigants to challenge inefficient law more often than efficient law.[13] These theories are provocative, though none has yet provided a sufficiently robust explanation of why or whether the common law is still efficient or more efficient than statutory laws. On the other hand, there is growing empirical evidence that common-law countries have higher economic growth rates than civil-law countries based on legal codes (such as France), and a negative correlation between the amount of regulation and economic growth, particularly in developing countries.[14]

---

13 P. Rubin, 'Why was the common law efficient?', Emory School of Law Working Paper no. 04-06, 2004; T. Zywicki, 'The rise and fall of efficiency in the common law: a supply-side analysis', *Northwestern Law Review*, 2003, 97: 1551–1663.

14 P. Mahoney, 'The common law and economic growth: Hayek might be right', *Journal of Legal Studies*, 2001, 30: 503–23.

Regulation as a barrier to competition

Governments do not have to create monopolies for regulation to reduce competition and consumer welfare. The ability of regulations to cause market failure and to redistribute income is often more subtle and less evident.

To illustrate, consider the way environmental and industrial safety legislation can create market power and enhance industry profits. The market-failure approach interprets such legislation as devices to deal with the inability of markets to provide adequate protection of workers, consumers and the public. This is often the stated intention of such legislation and assumed to be its effect. Yet empirical research often fails to find significant improvements in environmental quality and safety arising from such laws, but does paradoxically find that they increase industry costs substantially. A partial explanation lies in the type of laws implemented. Typically they impose technical and legal standards that the firm must observe and which focus on increasing safety/abatement inputs rather than deterring harms. For example, they require the employer to make capital expenditures such as purchasing machines with guards. This leads to two problems. First, often the mandated safety devices do not have an appreciable impact on the accident rate. There is a mismatch between the safety inputs that regulation requires or causes to be used, and those which most effectively control harmful activity. Thus the regulation, together with the firm's and workers' adaptive responses (see below), fails to achieve an appreciable reduction in the harm. At the same time the regulation raises the industry's costs.

The effects of such safety regulation do not stop there. It has indirect effects. If the regulation is stringent and vigorously enforced it raises a firm's costs and makes entry into the industry more difficult for the smaller firm. If firms have different compliance costs, owing to their size, location or the production process used, then regulation will have a more pronounced impact on some firms than others. This, in turn, will disadvantage those firms bearing higher costs, and the higher costs will act as a barrier to entry to new firms or the expansion of small firms. A number of empirical studies have confirmed this. A study of US industrial safety and environmental regulations by Bartel and Thomas[15] found that these raised the profits of industries with a high proportion of workers in large firms or in the 'frost belt', while those industries with a large number of small firms or located in the 'sun belt' lost profits. That is, they acted to give a competitive advantage to larger firms and those firms with more efficient technology. This is exactly the outcome that public choice theorists would predict – established, politically effective firms often lobby for legalistic command-and-control approaches to regulation specifically because they impose greater costs on competitors and enhance their profits, and this explains why industry is often hostile to tax and liability approaches, which would hit their profits immediately.

Adaptive responses to regulation

Another consideration often ignored in the analysis of regulation is the incentive or adaptive responses which lead to 'offsetting effects' and 'unintended consequences' that reduce its anticipated benefits or effects.

---

15   A. P. Bartel and L. C. Thomas, 'Predation through regulation: the wage and profit effects of the Occupational Safety and Health Administration and the Environmental Protection Agency', *Journal of Law and Economics*, 1987, 30: 239–65.

Economic theory predicts that individuals and organisations do not react passively to laws but adapt to the new price/cost configurations to minimise their adverse impact. That is, they will substitute cheaper activities to reduce the burden of the law. As a result it cannot be assumed that there is a one-to-one correspondence between the law, or what it requires, and what happens. The economist's simple incentive analysis indicates that actions will be taken which reduce the burden on those affected by a regulation or government policy. This may be in the desired direction, but it will also lead to offsetting effects.

A good example of this is the window tax. In order to raise revenues James I of England placed a tax on windows. The House and Window Duties Act 1766 imposed an annual tax of 3 shillings 15 pence on every house in England (and a lower sum in Scotland) and was progressive for houses with seven or more windows. Confronted with the window tax, the wealthy had three choices – pay the tax, evade the tax and/or have fewer windows. Many chose the last in order to reduce the taxes they had to pay. The architectural results are for all to see in London today – houses of that period with bricked-in windows. The consequence for the king was lower than expected tax revenues.

A more interesting example of an adaptive offsetting response is the reaction to compulsory seat-belt legislation. There is now fairly conclusive evidence that seat-belt laws have not had a significant impact on road safety. This is not because they are ineffective in protecting vehicle occupants but because they encourage risk-taking and accidents by drivers.

Road accidents are the result of the interaction of roads (their construction, topography, lighting and safety features), car design and use, and driver and pedestrian actions. As the roads and vehicles are made safer there is a natural inclination for drivers to take more risks by driving faster and less carefully, and braking too late. They substitute free, publicly provided road safety for costly, privately produced safety.

In the economic literature this effect was first recognised by Sam Peltzman[16] in his work on the impact of compulsory seat-belt legislation in the USA. He argued that because seat belts reduced driver risks and injuries, drivers adjusted their behaviour by driving faster and with less care. This led to fewer driver fatalities and more pedestrian fatalities and injuries, and damage to vehicles, thus increasing accident costs. The economics of the drivers' decision is simple to explain. A compulsory seat-belt requirement decreases the expected loss of an accident, and leads to offsetting risk-taking by more aggressive driving.

Peltzman tested this simple economic proposition using the US National Traffic and Motor Vehicle Safety Act 1966, which made the wearing of seat belts compulsory. Using statistical analysis, he found that occupant deaths per accident fell substantially as expected, but this reduction was entirely offset by more accidents to those not protected by seat belts, i.e. pedestrians and cyclists. While this finding was ridiculed at the time as fanciful, subsequent research by economists and traffic safety engineers has confirmed that compulsory seat-belt legislation has not resulted in a measurable decline in road fatalities.[17] Indeed, Peltzman[18] has revisited his original research to note that the

---

16   S. Peltzman, 'The effects of automobile safety regulation', *Journal of Political Economy*, 1975, 83: 677–725.

17   J. Adams, *Risk*, Routledge, London, 2005. This phenomenon has been identified independently by safety researchers as 'risk compensation'.

18   S. Peltzman, *Regulation and the Natural Progress of Opulence*, AEI-Brookings Joint Center for Regulatory Studies, Washington, DC, 2005.

annual rate of decline in highway deaths in the USA was 3.5 per cent from 1925 to 1960, before the legislation was enacted and at the height of Naderism; and between 1960 and 2004 it was also 3.5 per cent!

The theory of offsetting behaviour is evident in most command-and-control legislation. Minimum wage laws, rent controls (see above), sexual and racial discrimination laws and affirmative action laws all lead to adaptive or offsetting effects that reduce, sometimes substantially, their impact. Individuals and firms seek to minimise the costs that these laws impose, and this leads to a wider range of substitution effects, which may often not be in the desired or expected direction. The phenomenon extends well beyond regulation.[19] The computer was supposed to usher in the 'paperless office' but had the opposite effect of inundating offices with countless drafts and mountains of paper. There was a simple failure to recognise that the word-processor made drafting, editing and document production cheaper; and hence increased the number of drafts and paper copies.

Economics of legal rules

Another use of economics is to assist in the design and drafting of efficient or cost-effective legal rules and standards, and to identify the inefficiencies and distortive effects of existing and proposed legal approaches.

In theory, the efficiency of any system of legal rules requires a balancing of four principal costs:

---

19 For a more popular discussion, see E. Tenner, *Why Things Bite Back – New Technology and the Revenge Effect*, Fourth Estate, London, 1996.

- the costs of designing and implementing legal standards (rule-making costs);
- the costs of enforcing the standards (enforcement costs);
- the costs that they impose on the regulated industry (compliance costs); and
- the social costs imposed by regulatory offences.

Another cost associated with the legal system is error costs. Judges and regulators are not omniscient, nor do they correctly decide all cases. As a result they make Type I and Type II errors, or set out legal standards and rules that do not encourage efficient behaviour. Consider the former. A Type I error is where the court finds someone guilty when they are in fact not. A Type II error is where the court finds someone not guilty when they are guilty. Clearly when the courts commit such errors, they reduce the gains from complying with the law, and tend to alter the formal legal standards.

An 'efficient' system of enforcement is one that maximises the difference between the benefits and these costs and losses by selecting the appropriate type of rule, and level of enforcement.[20] This is obviously something easier said than done!

Steven Shavell has used a variant of the above approach to identify the factors relevant to the choice between *ex post* (liability rules) and *ex ante* safety regulation.[21] In his 'model' the choice of the optimal legal response depends on weighing four factors among victims and injurers:

20 I. Ehrlich and R. A. Posner, 'An economic analysis of legal rule-making', *Journal of Legal Studies*, 1974, 3: 257–86; S. Shavell, 'The optimal structure of law enforcement', *Journal of Law and Economics*, 1993, 36: 255–87.

21 S. Shavell, 'Liability for harm versus regulation of safety', *Journal of Legal Studies*, 1984, 13: 357–74.

- asymmetric information as regards risks;
- capacity of the injurer to pay, i.e. judgment proofness;
- probability of private suit; and
- relative magnitude of legal and regulatory costs.

Ex post responses, such as tort liability rules, are attractive if the victim is better informed, potential defendants (victims) can afford to pay claims, there is a high probability of suit should there be an actionable wrong, and legal process costs are low. Where these factors are weak, then public *ex ante* law techniques become more attractive, either as a replacement for the common law or as a complement.

The debate over *ex ante* and *ex post* legal responses has been a perennial one in safety regulation, but has become a more general concern in recent years. It has found new vitality in legal reform across Europe as the EU Commission and national governments grapple with the best way to regulate utilities – whether through antitrust laws (an *ex post* response) or *ex ante* sectoral regulation. The EU's New Regulatory Framework[22] for the regulation of the communications industry has seen an intense debate on whether the control of market power of telecommunications companies should rely on competition law or specially crafted price and access controls administered by sectoral regulators. The solution has been to develop *ex ante* responses based on competition law principles.[23]

---

22 *Directive 2002/21/EC on a common regulatory framework for electronic communications networks and services*, 24 April 2002.

23 See generally papers posted on the European Regulators' Group website (erg. eu.int), and C. G Veljanovski, *Remedies under EU Regulation of the Communications Sector*, Case Associates report prepared for European Telecommunications Network Operators' Association (ETNO), 20 June 2003.

Over-inclusive law

In practice many laws do not minimise social costs – they are either under- or over-inclusive. They can be under-inclusive when socially undesirable activities and practices are left unregulated. Other activities that are regulated are often subject to over-inclusive laws that prevent or deter activities thought to be socially desirable by setting standards that are too stringent, and/or compelling practices that are excessively costly and/or ineffective. A regulation is over-inclusive when the avoided social or external losses from complying with a standard are less than the sum of compliance and enforcement costs.

An example will serve to illustrate the idea. In the UK the speed limit in an urban area is 30 miles per hour. In general, this rule is a rough-and-ready way of ensuring adequate road safety. But in many specific instances it is not. The expectant father bundles his wife, who is about to give birth, into the family car and speeds to the local hospital. A policeman sees the speeding vehicle and stops it. Common sense tells us that rigidly enforcing the law in this case will do more harm than good – the rule is over-inclusive. Consider another example where full compliance can lead to counter-productive outcomes. Trade unions sometimes threaten to 'work to rule' as part of their negotiating strategy to gain concessions from employers in workplace disputes. This is regarded as a real threat since a legalistic and uncooperative interpretation of the rules by workers can lead to substantially reduced effort and workplace productivity.

Ignoring for the moment the claim made above that rules may not be intended to achieve efficiency, some degree of over-inclusion will inevitably arise from cost and information factors that make it impossible to devise the most effective intervention. For a regulation to be cost-effective, the standard-setting body (whether it be Parliament or a government department) must possess considerable information on the technological and economic conditions surrounding abatement and the degree of harm caused by hazards. The cost of collecting and processing this information will tend to limit the extent to which standards match the least-cost method of abatement. These information and implementation costs will tend to be greater the more complex, diverse and/or extensive the activity that is being controlled. In addition, the regulators will be involved in consultation with the regulated and interested parties, such as trade unions, giving rise to another set of costs (negotiation and consultation costs) and delay in the enactment of regulations.

The combination of these factors will lead to a regulatory framework that is often poorly matched to the cost-effective means of achieving regulatory objectives. Many breaches of the law will be technical ones that have very little to do with encouraging desirable behaviour or which achieve improvements at disproportionate cost. The problem of over-inclusion thus arises and will be accentuated over time, especially when changes in technology and economic conditions are rapid. As stated in the Robens Report, 'obsolescence is a chronic disease of the statutory safety provision'.[24]

Command-and-control regulation

The source of much regulatory cost and ineffectiveness is the technique of legal control. Much regulation is of the command-and-control variety: a law is established which sets out standards

---

24 Robens Report, *Committee on Safety and Health at Work*, Cmnd. 5034, HMSO, London, 1972, para. 29.

of conduct, usually controlling inputs rather than outcomes, which are publicly enforced by penalties and other sanctions. The effect of the legal rule enforced by criminal or civil sanctions presupposes that the rule is framed to avoid perverse incentive effects.

As already mentioned, much industrial safety legislation focuses on safety rather than on accidents. The employer is required to fit guards to machines or conform to certain safety practices under the threat of criminal prosecution. These control safety inputs rather than penalise the harm – accidents. Robert Smith summarises the economist's objections to this approach:

> First, standards may bear no relationship to the hazards in a particular operation, yet compliance (at whatever the cost) is mandatory. Second, by requiring a certain set of safety inputs rather than by penalising an unwanted outcome, such as injuries, the standards approach does not encourage firms to seek other perhaps cheaper ways of reducing injuries. Third, the promulgated standards are so numerous and workplaces so diverse, that one must question how comprehensive or knowledgeable inspections can be.[25]

It is also invariably the case that statutory regulations focus on those aspects of the problems which are easy to regulate rather than on the main causes of significant harms. For example, the English Factory Acts that historically controlled workplace safety and are still in force focused disproportionately on machinery accidents, despite the fact that many more accidents are the result of workers falling, slipping or mishandling objects.

25 R. S. Smith, 'The feasibility of an "injury tax" approach to occupational safety', *Law and Contemporary Problems*, 1974, 38: 730.

Over-inclusive regulation can lead to the paradox of increased compliance accompanied by little impact on controlling harms. Consider the following situation. The law controls a number of safety inputs that are relatively ineffective in reducing workplace accidents. These are enforced vigorously. The firm responds by complying, thus raising its costs. But it also rationally adapts to these increased costs by relaxing other aspects of workplace safety which are not subject to regulation and which may be more effect-ive in reducing accidents. This may result in higher costs without fewer accidents. Resources are simply channelled into compliance with ineffective laws, rather than into preventing accidents in the most effective way.

This type of adaptive response is graphically illustrated by a case unearthed by Kagan and Schulz[26] in their study of the enforce-ment of industrial safety regulation by the US Occupational Safety and Health Administration (OSHA). A steel company became embroiled in disputes with OSHA, which during the 1970s adopted an aggressive enforcement policy. One of the firm's immediate responses to what it regarded as unreasonable persecu-tions by OSHA was to sack the trained safety engineer who headed its accident-prevention programme and replace him with a lawyer charged with litigating OSHA prosecutions. This outcome is a clear example where the response was to substitute one input for another (in this case to deal with regulation) that was less effective in reducing harm and improving worker welfare.

Thus, under legalistic modes of regulation a situation can arise where increased enforcement leads to greater compliance and higher costs for some firms, but because firms have adapted

26 R. A. Kagan and J. T. Scholz, in K. Hawkins and J. M. Thomas (eds), *Enforcing Regulation*, Kluwer-Nijhoff, Boston, MA, 1984, ch. 4.

to this constraint by relaxing other aspects of workplace safety, accidents do not fall and may even increase. The odd thing is that the regulator can claim success – after all, has not the level of enforcement and prosecutions increased and have not more firms complied with safety laws? Yet looking behind these official statistics, we see the costs to industry rising, and workers bewildered by the fact that there has been no appreciable increase in job safety.

Dealing with over-inclusion

There are several ways of dealing with the problem of over-inclusive regulation.

The first is to abandon the traditional command-and-control approach and rely on incentive regulation and market solutions such as creating property rights and markets (emission rights markets), pricing (such as congestion charging) and fiscal sanctions (e.g. a pollution tax). These are considered briefly later.

The second is to devote more resources to framing efficient laws. One option is to use cost–benefit analysis as an integral part of the lawmaking process, and to require that estimated benefits exceed costs. This is also considered below.

The third is to use standards rather than prescriptive legal rules. This approach has already been discussed in relation to negligence, where legal intervention is based on a judgmental or cost–benefit standard that balances costs and benefits. That is, instead of the law simply requiring the adoption of certain practices and inputs, it makes the firm's liability contingent on breaching a cost–benefit standard. Such a standard would effectively adopt fault liability or the Hand Test to impose the law and/or guide its enforcement through the exercise of discretion

by regulators and courts. This has been a feature of English industrial safety legislation, which bases the employer's culpability on
the notion of 'reasonably practicable' – a statutory test found
in the Factory Acts and as old as the common law of employers'
liability.[27] In the leading modern case of *Edwards v The National
Coal Board*, the Court of Appeal held that:

> 'reasonably practicable' … seems to me to imply that a
> computation must be made by the owner in which the
> quantum of risk is placed on one scale and the sacrifice
> involved in the measures necessary for averting the risk
> (whether in money, time or trouble) is placed in the other,
> and that, if it be shown that there is a gross disproportion
> between them – the risk being insignificant in relation to the
> sacrifice – the defendants discharge the onus on them.[28]

Another approach is to give regulators discretion and to allow
them to negotiate compliance so that cost and risk factors can be
taken into account on a case-by-case basis. Political scientists have
noted that some regulators use 'negotiated compliance' rather
than a penalty approach to law enforcement in order to conserve
enforcement resources,[29] and target enforcement efforts on those
rules which are cost effective in reducing harms. This may or may
not be efficient depending on the conditions surrounding the
enforcement and penalty structures.

---

27 C. Veljanovski, 'Regulatory enforcement – an economic case study of the British
 Factory Inspectorate', *Law and Policy Quarterly*, 1983, 5: 75–96.

28 [1949] 1 KB 704; [1949] 1 All ER 743. See Health & Safety Executive, 'Principles and
 guidelines to assist HSE in its judgements that duty holders have reduced risk as
 low as reasonably practicable', at www.hse.gov.uk/risk/theory/a;arp1.htm.

29 P. Fenn and C. Veljanovski, 'A positive economic theory of regulatory enforcement', *Economic Journal*, 1988, 98: 1055–70, reprinted in Ogus (ed.), *Regulation,
 Economics and the Law*, op. cit.

Use of cost–benefit analysis

Risk assessment and cost–benefit analysis of regulation are now fashionable.[30] Many governments beginning with that of the USA[31] have implemented schemes to subject new regulation to cost–benefit assessments, and have set up 'deregulation units' to cut red tape and the regulatory 'burden on business'. For example, the Financial Services Act 1988, which was originally not subject to any cost–benefit assessment, is now, after two decades.[32]

Using cost assessments and cost–benefit analysis of regulation is not new. The Thatcher government's Compliance Cost Assessment (CCA) system required all central government departments to identify the costs of each proposed regulation, but had little effect. The Major government revamped the process with the Deregulation and Contracting Out Act 1994, and the Blair government continued this effort with the Regulatory Reform Act 2001 and Regulatory Impact Assessments (RIAs). All proposed regulations in the UK today must be accompanied by an RIA, which sets out the objective, the risks, the options, the costs and benefits, and the competitive impact and other matters. The RIA must indicate that estimated benefits justify the costs, or at least are proportionate, although this is not a legal requirement. It also must contain a signed ministerial declaration stating: 'I have read the Regulatory Impact Assessment and I am satisfied that the benefits justify the costs.'

---

30 C. R. Sunstein, *Risk and Reason – Safety, Law and the Environment*, Cambridge University Press, Cambridge, 2002.

31 R. Baldwin and C. G. Veljanovski, 'Regulation by cost–benefit analysis', *Public Administration*, 1984, 62: 51–69.

32 I. Alfon and P. Andrews, *Cost–Benefit Analysis in Financial Regulation*, FSA Occasional Papers in Financial Regulation no. 3, 1999.

Viewed objectively, these efforts have not been a success. The RIAs, and similar efforts, often are no more than form-filling exercises in support of a government department's preferred legalistic approach, rather than genuine attempts to identify the most efficient regulation.[33] Past attempts have been acknowledged as failures. Paradoxically, the proposed Legislative and Regulatory Reform Bill in early 2006 (subsequently withdrawn) has emerged as a challenge to parliamentary democracy, giving ministers (the executive branch) the legal powers to introduce and modify legislation.

Even at a practical technical level of assessing regulation the effort has fallen far short of its own limited objectives. The superficiality of the government's costing exercises can be illustrated by one RIA selected at random from the UK Department for Transport's website on the highly topical subject of banning the use of hand-held mobile (cell) phones while driving.[34] In the UK it is now an offence to use a hand-held mobile phone, and there are moves to tighten up the legislation.

The 'mobile' RIA has the attraction of brevity, but this unfortunately reflects superficiality rather succinct analysis. It is thin on facts and strong on assumptions, many of which are implausible. Let us just consider some. The RIA claims that there is evidence that mobile phone use causes additional accidents but does not quantify the enhanced risks. It states that a 1 per cent reduction in road casualties in 2001 would avoid costs of £118 million, using the

---

33 National Audit Office, *Evaluation of Regulatory Impact Assessments Compendium*, Report 2003-04, 4 March 2004; R. W. Hahn and P. Dudley, *How Well Does the Government Do Cost–benefit Analysis?*, Working Paper 04-01, AEI-Brookings Joint Center for Regulatory Studies, Washington, DC, 2004.

34 Department for Transport, *Mobile Phones and Driving – Offence of using a hand-held mobile phone while driving*, RIA, 20 October 2003.

department's standard valuations of injury and fatalities, which include a measure for the WTP (willingness to pay) for statistical life and injury under the heading 'human costs',[35] as shown in Table 2.

Table 2 **Average value of prevention per casualty by severity and element of cost (£ June 2003)**

Injury severity	Lost output	Medical and ambulance	Human costs	TOTAL
Fatal	451,110	770	860,380	1,312,260
Serious	17,380	10,530	119,550	147,460
Slight	1,840	780	8,750	11,370
Average, all casualties	9,060	1,910	31,880	42,850

This is clearly intended to be read as a claim that the new regulation will result in these savings, otherwise the calculations are meaningless. Remarkably, the RIA is based on the assumption that no additional police resources will be involved in enforcing the law – enforcement will take place as part of the existing 'normal traffic policing duties'. The new offence is estimated to result in 50,000–100,000 fixed penalty charges, generating fine revenues of £1.5–£3 million, and additional court costs to a maximum of £3 million. Thus, the fines and additional court costs cancel each other out, and the ban generates suggested 'benefits' of in excess of £118 million.

It does not take a genius, or even an economist, to appreciate that this RIA is deeply flawed. First, it does not link the enforcement of

---

35 Department for Transport, *2003 Valuation of the Benefits of Prevention of Road Accidents and Casualties*, Highways Economics Note no. 1, 2004; D. J. Ball, D. P. Ives and I. G. Wilson, *The Optimisation of Consumer Safety: A report on behalf of Department of Trade and Industry's Consumer Safety Unit*, October 1997.

the law to compliance, and compliance with the law to the assumed reduction in accidents. It makes an assumption not backed up by any evidence that 1 per cent of accidents will be avoided annually, and assumes total (100 per cent) compliance with the law. It notes that hands-free mobile devices can still be legally used, but the RIA states that the department is against the in-car use of any mobile phones. It refers to cost estimates for hands-free sets and their installation, but does not take these into account in costing the hand-held ban. Thus, the RIA does not assess the proposed regulation but a total ban on in-car mobile phone use.

Even ignoring this, the RIA does not critically evaluate the experimental and other evidence of the relationship between mobile-phone use and traffic accidents. For example, we know that in the research cited in the RIA there are selectivity biases because users of mobile phones are more likely to engage in other (substitutable) risk-taking actions when driving. So the experimental and observed evidence of the risks posed by mobile-phone use in vehicles is likely to overestimate the true risks associated with mobile-phone use, and, consequently, the extent of accident reduction as a result of a ban on hand-held mobiles. This simply reiterates the point already stressed about adaptive behaviour, which may partially offset the anticipated gains in risk reduction. A driver not able to make a mobile call from his vehicle to say he or she is late may drive more aggressively when the ban is effectively enforced and increase the risk of other types of accidents. Thus, the gains in terms of avoided risk-taking, material losses and physical injuries will be less. Second, the analysis ignores the gains from mobile-phone usage.[36] Presumably drivers benefit from

36   R. W. Hahn and P. M. Dudley, 'The disconnect between law and policy analysis – a case study of drivers and cell phones', *Administrative Law Review*, 2003, 55: 127–83.

using mobiles in cars and a value should have been put on these gains, as it should on the costs of installing hands-free equipment in vehicles to comply with the law.

Third, the RIA assumes that a 1 per cent reduction or full compliance with the law can be achieved within the existing police budget. While the RIA does not translate this into the number of avoided accidents by category, these can be inferred from its estimates of costs savings (Table 3). The reality will be only partial compliance (and therefore far less than the predicted reduction in accidents), and to the extent that the ban is enforced it will divert resources away from other traffic offences and police duties. In the absence of more resources given to the police, this means an increase in other traffic offences, or other crimes, and hence a lower than predicted net gain.

In summary, the mobile phone RIA evaluates the wrong law, does not analyse it, or the right law's impact, ignores significant categories of costs, especially as they pertain to motorists, and contains simplistic analysis of the benefits of the law, so that one may seriously wonder whether it has added anything to 'better regulation'. This is not surprising, since simple public choice theory would indicate that unless the bureaucratic and political incentives within government encourage proper costing, the pursuit of efficient regulation will be weak!

Table 3 **Estimated annual cost savings from mobile phone ban (2001 £ prices)**

Type of accident	Valuation	Total value (£ million)	No. of avoided accidents
Fatalities	1,190,000	41.00	34
Serious injuries	134,000	49.75	371
Slight injuries	10,000	27.25	2,725

Market-based alternatives

The obvious remedy to many of the problems identified above is to abandon the command-and-control approach and adopt market solutions or market-based regulation. These vary over a spectrum of techniques that focus on outcomes rather than inputs, and seek to give firms and individuals incentives to adopt cost-effective solutions. Among the techniques available are creating private property rights and markets, auctions, pricing and fiscal incentives (taxes and subsidies).

Creating markets is the most obvious response to many areas where direct regulation is currently used. This can take the form of creating and enforcing property rights in previously unowned resources and assets. This in turn harnesses the profit motive to prevent over-exploitation and husband natural resources.

Consider the plight of the African elephant. The regulatory response is to have state-run National Parks, and a militia protect the elephants from being shot by poachers. The government can respond to increased poaching (which is a product of the world demand for ivory) by making the penalties for poaching draconian and burning any confiscated ivory. But this in the end only sends the market price of ivory soaring and increases the gains from poaching. An alternative response is to privatise the elephants. If elephant farms were permitted, normal economic forces would ensure that these precious beasts were not poached to extinction. This type of response is happening in Africa.

In other cases pseudo-markets can be set up, such as tradable pollution or emission rights. For example, marketable emission or pollution permits can be issued to firms up to the level of the desired cutback. The permits can then be traded. This creates a market in pollution in which firms who find it unprofitable to reduce the level of, say, toxic emissions sell permits to other firms that can achieve reductions at low cost or which value the right to pollute very highly. In this way the desired reduction in pollution is achieved in the least costly way.

Market solutions are being used in other areas, such as radio spectrum. From the 1920s until recently it was firmly believed that a market in spectrum was not possible, giving rise to inefficient uses and radio interference. Thus the amount and use of spectrum had to be rationed and strictly regulated. Today, there is an appreciation that the reason why early markets in spectrum appeared to fail was because of the absence of enforceable property rights, which, as with roads, led to congestion as users in commercially attractive bands used the same spectrum. Today the use of market solutions has become accepted, but not as yet a fully fledged market in spectrum.[37] Across Europe and elsewhere auctions have been used to allocate spectrum to third-generation (3G) mobile phones. This has the attraction of being a more transparent and fairer way of allocating spectrum than the previous 'beauty parades' based on administrative and technical criteria, and of course has raised considerable sums of money for governments. Further, reforms are afoot to extend the use of markets to allow limited trading in spectrum, known as secondary trading, in the UK[38] and Europe, as has already been implemented in New Zealand and Australia.

---

37 First proposed in 1951 by a law student at the University of Chicago, and later used by Coase to set out the Coase Theorem; L. Herzel, 'Public interest and the market in color television', *University of Chicago Law Review*, 1951, 18: 802–16; R. H. Coase, 'The Federal Communications Commission', *Journal of Law and Economics*, 1959, 2: 1–40.

38 *Review of Radio Spectrum Management – an independent Review for Department of Trade and Industry & HM Treasury* (chair Professor Martin Cave), March 2002.

One country that has gone farther by embracing a market solution has been Guatemala, under its telecommunications law of 1995. Spectrum rights there have been assigned on a first-in-time basis for uses determined by those filing claims with the regulatory agency. Those who have secured spectrum rights can negotiate 'change of use' subject to pre-defined technical limits designed to minimise technical interference. This market-determined approach appears to be working well.[39]

Another solution is to use prices to ration usage and guide investment. The use of prices has been advocated for many years by economists to deal with road congestion and pollution. The adoption has been hindered by political resistance and the absence of a technology that would enable a pricing scheme. As the volume of traffic and congestion in urban areas have increased, however, governments have been forced to seek solutions rather than endlessly attempt to build themselves out of congestion. Singapore paved the way, and recently congestion charges implemented in central London have reduced the volume of traffic.

The last approach is fiscal instruments. A regime of taxes is implemented which reflect the social costs that a harmful activity imposes on society. Thus, instead of having environmental controls, a 'pollution tax' is imposed on some measure of emission or some variable positively correlated with the level of pollution, such as units of output sold. By imposing a tax on pollution or injuries that approximates the uncompensated losses imposed on other individuals, the industry is left to decide whether clean-up is cost-effective and in what ways it can be undertaken. Taxes must ideally be placed on the undesirable activity that one is seeking

---

39   P. T. Spiller and C. Cardilli, 'Toward a property right approach to communications spectrum', *Yale Journal of Regulation*, 1999, 16: 75–81.

to internalise or deter. For example, if one wants to encourage a cost-effective reduction in pollution, the ideal tax is an emission or pollution tax which is placed on the harmful output or activity. Imposing a tax on cars is not efficient since it does not take into account the level of emission of different cars, nor does it encourage the adoption of less polluting engines. Thus the choice of the tax base and the tax level are important, as are the enforcement costs.

The above discussion of the attractions of market solutions must be qualified. The mere fact that a market-type approach has been adopted does not guarantee its efficiency or effectiveness. This is because government still plays a large role in setting the number of tradable permits, the definition of initial property rights and the tax base and rates. Often these are inappropriately set. A recent example of 'government failure' in this area was in 2006, when it emerged that some EU member states (e.g. Germany) had issued permits allowing more carbon emission than the level of CO_2 produced by their industries. The result was no expected reduction in CO_2 emissions and market chaos as the price of the tradable emission rights halved from a peak of €30 to €12 per tonne over several days in April 2006. The auction of spectrum licences is another example. While this can place the available spectrum in the hands of those who value it most, the use, amount and parcelling of spectrum among users is determined by government, and trading in spectrum is limited. Thus while an auction and a secondary market can make a good job of a bad situation, the overall outcome may still be far from efficient.

8   CONCLUDING REMARKS

Laws exist for a purpose; they are not ends in themselves. They seek to guide, control, deter and punish. It follows that the study of law must, almost by definition, be broadened to include an understanding of its justification and effects. As Lon Fuller observed, law 'is the only human study having no distinctive end of its own. Where its ends can be regarded as grounded in reason, and not brute expressions of political power, those ends must be derived not from law itself but from ethics, sociology and economics'.[1]

In my view, economics comes at the top of any wider study of law for several straightforward reasons. First, it has a well-developed theory that is widely accepted by the economics profession. Most other social sciences cannot make this claim. Second, economics plays such an important part in the operation of the law that it would be foolhardy to ignore the subject. Laws impose and shift costs; they are costly, they create incentives and they alter behaviour. Third, even if we do not accept that economic factors are important, we still need to know *how much* our preconceived ideas of rights, justice and morality are costing. Often the simple application of economics can reveal hidden and inconsistent assumptions and generate useful insights. This view is shared by Holmes, one of the greatest US judges, who over a century ago

---

1   L. L. Fuller, *Anatomy of Law*, Praeger, New York, 1968, p. 4.

looked forward to the ideal state of legal education, where the legal scholar's energy was directed to the

> … study of the ends sought to be attained and the reasons for desiring them. As a step toward that ideal it seems to me that every lawyer ought to seek an understanding of economics. The present divorce between the schools of political economy and law seems to me evidence of how much progress in philosophical study still remains to be made. In … political economy … we are called on to consider and weigh the ends of legislation, the means of attaining them, and the cost. We learn that for everything we have to give up something else, and we are taught to set the advantage we gain against the other advantage we lose, and to know what we are doing when we elect.[2]

And if this were not enough reward, Holmes believed that the lawyer who studies economics will not only become a better lawyer but a happier and much wiser person:

> … happiness, I am sure from having known many successful men, cannot be won simply by being counsel for great corporations and having an income of fifty thousand dollars. An intellect great enough to win the prize needs other food besides success. It is through [the study of the remoter and more general aspects of the law] … that you not only become a great master in your calling, but connect your subject with the universe and catch an echo of the infinite, a glimpse of its unfathomable process, a hint of the universal law.[3]

---

2 O. W. Holmes, 'The path of the law', *Harvard Law Review*, 1897, 10: 474.

3 Ibid., p. 478.

QUESTIONS FOR DISCUSSION

1. Identify the differences between economic and legal reasoning.
2. Why has economics been applied to the analysis of law and regulation?
3. Discuss the claim that lawyers are interested in justice, while economists are preoccupied with economic efficiency.
4. What is the link between costs and benefits, on the one hand, and the way laws affect individual behaviour, on the other?
5. What is the Coase Theorem? Discuss its importance for the economic analysis of law.
6. Does the legal notion of 'reasonable care' have an economic definition?
7. Why do economists prefer fines as a criminal sanction?
8. How has economics contributed to the definition of a market and effective competition, terms found in competition laws?
9. Discuss the different theories of regulation.
10. What is rent-seeking?

FURTHER READING

Barzel, Y., *Economic Analysis of Property Rights*, 2nd edn, Cambridge University Press, Cambridge, 1997.

Bouckaert, B. and G. De Geest (eds), *Encyclopedia of Law and Economics*, Edward Elgar, Cheltenham, 2000 (free version at http://encyclo.findlaw.com/index.html).

Cooter, R. and T. Ulen, *Law and Economics*, 4th edn, Pearson Addison Wesley, Boston, MA, 2004.

Dau-Schmidt, K. G. and T. S. Ulen (eds), *Law and Economics Anthology*, Anderson Publishing Co., 2002.

Friedman, D. D., *Law's Order: What Economics Has to Do with the Law and Why It Matters*, Princeton University Press, Princeton, NJ, 2000.

Newman, P. (ed.), *The New Palgrave Dictionary of Economics and the Law*, 3 vols, Stockton Press, London, 1998.

Ogus, A. I. (ed.), *Regulation, Economics and the Law*, Edward Elgar, Cheltenham, 2001.

Polinsky, A. M., *An Introduction to the Economics of Law*, 3rd edn, Aspen Publishers, New York, 2003.

Posner, R. A., *Economic Analysis of Law*, 6th edn, Aspen Publishers, New York, 2003.

Shavell, S., *Foundations of the Economic Analysis of Law*, Harvard University Press, Cambridge, MA, 2004.

Veljanovski, C. G., *Economic Principles of Law*, Cambridge University Press, Cambridge, 2007 (in press).

Williamson, O. E., *The Economic Institutions of Capitalism*, Free Press, New York, 1985.

Wittman, D. (ed.), *Readings in the Economic Analysis of the Law*, Blackwell, Oxford, 2002.

ABOUT THE IEA

The Institute is a research and educational charity (No. CC 235 351), limited by guarantee. Its mission is to improve understanding of the fundamental institutions of a free society by analysing and expounding the role of markets in solving economic and social problems.

The IEA achieves its mission by:

- a high-quality publishing programme
- conferences, seminars, lectures and other events
- outreach to school and college students
- brokering media introductions and appearances

The IEA, which was established in 1955 by the late Sir Antony Fisher, is an educational charity, not a political organisation. It is independent of any political party or group and does not carry on activities intended to affect support for any political party or candidate in any election or referendum, or at any other time. It is financed by sales of publications, conference fees and voluntary donations.

In addition to its main series of publications the IEA also publishes a quarterly journal, *Economic Affairs*.

The IEA is aided in its work by a distinguished international Academic Advisory Council and an eminent panel of Honorary Fellows. Together with other academics, they review prospective IEA publications, their comments being passed on anonymously to authors. All IEA papers are therefore subject to the same rigorous independent refereeing process as used by leading academic journals.

IEA publications enjoy widespread classroom use and course adoptions in schools and universities. They are also sold throughout the world and often translated/reprinted.

Since 1974 the IEA has helped to create a world-wide network of 100 similar institutions in over 70 countries. They are all independent but share the IEA's mission.

Views expressed in the IEA's publications are those of the authors, not those of the Institute (which has no corporate view), its Managing Trustees, Academic Advisory Council members or senior staff.

Members of the Institute's Academic Advisory Council, Honorary Fellows, Trustees and Staff are listed on the following page.

The Institute gratefully acknowledges financial support for its publications programme and other work from a generous benefaction by the late Alec and Beryl Warren.

The Institute of Economic Affairs
2 Lord North Street, Westminster, London SW1P 3LB
Tel: 020 7799 8900
Fax: 020 7799 2137
Email: iea@iea.org.uk
Internet: iea.org.uk

Other papers recently published by the IEA include:

The World Turned Rightside Up

A New Trading Agenda for the Age of Globalisation
John C. Hulsman
Occasional Paper 114; ISBN 0 255 36495 4
£8.00

The Representation of Business in English Literature

Introduced and edited by Arthur Pollard
Readings 53; ISBN 0 255 36491 1
£12.00

Anti-Liberalism 2000

The Rise of New Millennium Collectivism
David Henderson
Occasional Paper 115; ISBN 0 255 36497 0
£7.50

Capitalism, Morality and Markets

Brian Griffiths, Robert A. Sirico, Norman Barry & Frank Field
Readings 54; ISBN 0 255 36496 2
£7.50

A Conversation with Harris and Seldon

Ralph Harris & Arthur Seldon
Occasional Paper 116; ISBN 0 255 36498 9
£7.50

Malaria and the DDT Story

Richard Tren & Roger Bate
Occasional Paper 117; ISBN 0 255 36499 7
£10.00

A Plea to Economists Who Favour Liberty:
Assist the Everyman

Daniel B. Klein
Occasional Paper 118; ISBN 0 255 36501 2
£10.00

The Changing Fortunes of Economic Liberalism

Yesterday, Today and Tomorrow
David Henderson
Occasional Paper 105 (new edition); ISBN 0 255 36520 9
£12.50

The Global Education Industry

Lessons from Private Education in Developing Countries
James Tooley
Hobart Paper 141 (new edition); ISBN 0 255 36503 9
£12.50

Saving Our Streams

*The Role of the Anglers' Conservation Association in
Protecting English and Welsh Rivers*
Roger Bate
Research Monograph 53; ISBN 0 255 36494 6
£10.00

Better Off Out?

The Benefits or Costs of EU Membership
Brian Hindley & Martin Howe
Occasional Paper 99 (new edition); ISBN 0 255 36502 0
£10.00

Buckingham at 25

Freeing the Universities from State Control
Edited by James Tooley
Readings 55; ISBN 0 255 36512 8
£15.00

Lectures on Regulatory and Competition Policy

Irwin M. Stelzer
Occasional Paper 120; ISBN 0 255 36511 X
£12.50

Misguided Virtue

False Notions of Corporate Social Responsibility
David Henderson
Hobart Paper 142; ISBN 0 255 36510 1
£12.50

HIV and Aids in Schools

The Political Economy of Pressure Groups and Miseducation
Barrie Craven, Pauline Dixon, Gordon Stewart & James Tooley
Occasional Paper 121; ISBN 0 255 36522 5
£10.00

The Road to Serfdom

The Reader's Digest *condensed version*
Friedrich A. Hayek
Occasional Paper 122; ISBN 0 255 36530 6
£7.50

Bastiat's *The Law*

Introduction by Norman Barry
Occasional Paper 123; ISBN 0 255 36509 8
£7.50

A Globalist Manifesto for Public Policy

Charles Calomiris
Occasional Paper 124; ISBN 0 255 36525 X
£7.50

Euthanasia for Death Duties

Putting Inheritance Tax Out of Its Misery
Barry Bracewell-Milnes
Research Monograph 54; ISBN 0 255 36513 6
£10.00

Liberating the Land

The Case for Private Land-use Planning
Mark Pennington
Hobart Paper 143; ISBN 0 255 36508 X
£10.00

IEA Yearbook of Government Performance 2002/2003
Edited by Peter Warburton
Yearbook 1; ISBN 0 255 36532 2
£15.00

Britain's Relative Economic Performance, 1870–1999
Nicholas Crafts
Research Monograph 55; ISBN 0 255 36524 1
£10.00

Should We Have Faith in Central Banks?
Otmar Issing
Occasional Paper 125; ISBN 0 255 36528 4
£7.50

The Dilemma of Democracy
Arthur Seldon
Hobart Paper 136 (reissue); ISBN 0 255 36536 5
£10.00

Capital Controls: a 'Cure' Worse Than the Problem?
Forrest Capie
Research Monograph 56; ISBN 0 255 36506 3
£10.00

The Poverty of 'Development Economics'
Deepak Lal
Hobart Paper 144 (reissue); ISBN 0 255 36519 5
£15.00

Should Britain Join the Euro?

The Chancellor's Five Tests Examined
Patrick Minford
Occasional Paper 126; ISBN 0 255 36527 6
£7.50

Post-Communist Transition: Some Lessons

Leszek Balcerowicz
Occasional Paper 127; ISBN 0 255 36533 0
£7.50

A Tribute to Peter Bauer

John Blundell et al.
Occasional Paper 128; ISBN 0 255 36531 4
£10.00

Employment Tribunals

Their Growth and the Case for Radical Reform
J. R. Shackleton
Hobart Paper 145; ISBN 0 255 36515 2
£10.00

Fifty Economic Fallacies Exposed

Geoffrey E. Wood
Occasional Paper 129; ISBN 0 255 36518 7
£12.50

A Market in Airport Slots

Keith Boyfield (editor), David Starkie, Tom Bass & Barry Humphreys
Readings 56; ISBN 0 255 36505 5
£10.00

Money, Inflation and the Constitutional Position of the Central Bank

Milton Friedman & Charles A. E. Goodhart

Readings 57; ISBN 0 255 36538 1

£10.00

railway.com

Parallels between the Early British Railways and the ICT Revolution

Robert C. B. Miller

Research Monograph 57; ISBN 0 255 36534 9

£12.50

The Regulation of Financial Markets

Edited by Philip Booth & David Currie

Readings 58; ISBN 0 255 36551 9

£12.50

Climate Alarmism Reconsidered

Robert L. Bradley Jr

Hobart Paper 146; ISBN 0 255 36541 1

£12.50

Government Failure: E. G. West on Education

Edited by James Tooley & James Stanfield

Occasional Paper 130; ISBN 0 255 36552 7

£12.50

Waging the War of Ideas

John Blundell

Second edition

Occasional Paper 131; ISBN 0 255 36547 0

£12.50

Corporate Governance: Accountability in the Marketplace
Elaine Sternberg
Second edition
Hobart Paper 147; ISBN 0 255 36542 X
£12.50

The Land Use Planning System
Evaluating Options for Reform
John Corkindale
Hobart Paper 148; ISBN 0 255 36550 0
£10.00

Economy and Virtue
Essays on the Theme of Markets and Morality
Edited by Dennis O'Keeffe
Readings 59; ISBN 0 255 36504 7
£12.50

Free Markets Under Siege
Cartels, Politics and Social Welfare
Richard A. Epstein
Occasional Paper 132; ISBN 0 255 36553 5
£10.00

Unshackling Accountants
D. R. Myddelton
Hobart Paper 149; ISBN 0 255 36559 4
£12.50

The Euro as Politics

Pedro Schwartz

Research Monograph 58; ISBN 0 255 36535 7

£12.50

Pricing Our Roads

Vision and Reality

Stephen Glaister & Daniel J. Graham

Research Monograph 59; ISBN 0 255 36562 4

£10.00

The Role of Business in the Modern World

Progress, Pressures, and Prospects for the Market Economy

David Henderson

Hobart Paper 150; ISBN 0 255 36548 9

£12.50

Public Service Broadcasting Without the BBC?

Alan Peacock

Occasional Paper 133; ISBN 0 255 36565 9

£10.00

The ECB and the Euro: the First Five Years

Otmar Issing

Occasional Paper 134; ISBN 0 255 36555 1

£10.00

Towards a Liberal Utopia?

Edited by Philip Booth

Hobart Paperback 32; ISBN 0 255 36563 2

£15.00

The Way Out of the Pensions Quagmire
Philip Booth & Deborah Cooper
Research Monograph 60; ISBN 0 255 36517 9
£12.50

Black Wednesday
A Re-examination of Britain's Experience in the Exchange Rate Mechanism
Alan Budd
Occasional Paper 135; ISBN 0 255 36566 7
£7.50

Crime: Economic Incentives and Social Networks
Paul Ormerod
Hobart Paper 151; ISBN 0 255 36554 3
£10.00

The Road to Serfdom *with* The Intellectuals and Socialism
Friedrich A. Hayek
Occasional Paper 136; ISBN 0 255 36576 4
£10.00

Money and Asset Prices in Boom and Bust
Tim Congdon
Hobart Paper 152; ISBN 0 255 36570 5
£10.00

The Dangers of Bus Re-regulation
and Other Perspectives on Markets in Transport
John Hibbs et al.
Occasional Paper 137; ISBN 0 255 36572 1
£10.00

The New Rural Economy

Change, Dynamism and Government Policy
Berkeley Hill et al.
Occasional Paper 138; ISBN 0 255 36546 2
£15.00

The Benefits of Tax Competition

Richard Teather
Hobart Paper 153; ISBN 0 255 36569 1
£12.50

Wheels of Fortune

Self-funding Infrastructure and the Free Market Case for a Land Tax
Fred Harrison
Hobart Paper 154; ISBN 0 255 36589 6
£12.50

Were 364 Economists All Wrong?

Edited by Philip Booth
Readings 60
ISBN-10: 0 255 36588 8; ISBN-13: 978 0 255 36588 8
£10.00

Europe After the 'No' Votes

Mapping a New Economic Path
Patrick A. Messerlin
Occasional Paper 139
ISBN-10: 0 255 36580 2; ISBN-13: 978 0 255 36580 2
£10.00

The Railways, the Market and the Government

John Hibbs et al.
Readings 61
ISBN-10: 0 255 36567 5; ISBN-13: 978 0 255 36567 3
£12.50

Choice and the End of Social Housing

Peter King
Hobart Paper 155
ISBN-10: 0 255 36568 3; ISBN-13: 978 0 255 36568 0
£10.00

Corruption – The World's Big C

Cases, Causes, Consequences, Cures
Ian Senior
Research Monograph 61
ISBN-10: 0 255 36571 3; ISBN-13: 978 0 255 36571 0
£12.50

Sir Humphrey's Legacy

Facing Up to the Cost of Public Sector Pensions
Neil Record
Hobart Paper 156
ISBN-10: 0 255 36578 0; ISBN-13: 978 0 255 36578 9
£10.00

To order copies of currently available IEA papers, or to enquire about availability, please contact:

Gazelle
IEA orders
FREEPOST RLYS-EAHU-YSCZ
White Cross Mills
Hightown
Lancaster LA1 4XS

Tel: 01524 68765
Fax: 01524 63232
Email: sales@gazellebooks.co.uk

The IEA also offers a subscription service to its publications. For a single annual payment, currently £40.00 in the UK, you will receive every monograph the IEA publishes during the course of a year and discounts on our extensive back catalogue. For more information, please contact:

Adam Myers
Subscriptions
The Institute of Economic Affairs
2 Lord North Street
London SW1P 3LB

Tel: 020 7799 8920
Fax: 020 7799 2137
Website: www.iea.org.uk